CW01551773

YOUNG WRITERS

OVER THE MOON

NORFOLK

published in Great Britain in 1996 by
POETRY NOW
1-2 Wainman Road, Woodston,
Peterborough, PE2 7BU

All Rights Reserved

HB ISBN 1 86188 038 3
SB ISBN 1 86188 033 2

Foreword

The *Over The Moon* competition was an overwhelming success - over 43,000 entries were received from 8-11 year olds up and down the country, all written on a wide variety of subjects. Reading all these poems has been a painstaking task - but very enjoyable.

Many of the poems were beautifully illustrated. This just emphasises how much time, effort and thought was put into the work. For me, this makes the editing process so much harder.

I hope that *Over The Moon Norfolk* highlights the diversity of today's young minds. I believe that each of these poems shows a great deal of creativity and imagination. Many of them also express an understanding of the problems, socially and environmentally, that we are all facing.

The poems that follow are all written on different levels, and some are more light-hearted than others. With a considerable variety of subjects and styles, there should be something to appeal to everyone.

Sarah Andrew
Editor

CONTENTS

Rachel Sage	21
Lisa Stearman	22
Scott Townsend	22
Clare Walker	23
Tom Skoyles	23
Lisa Rogers	24
Simon Welfare	24
Jeremy Wright	25
Lawrence Owen	26
Mark Fox	26
Beth Jex	27
Laura Davies	27
Alice Lupton	28
Ben Hepworth	28
Claire Foster	29
Rebecca Botwright	29
Robert Slaughter	30
Joe Houchen	30
Joe Riches	31

Beeston Hall School

Kate Creelman	31
Artem Kossenko	32
Tim Wilson	32
Louise Watson	33
David Abbott	33
Tom Clabburn	34
Zoe Sallon	35
Hannah Marsh	36
James Carter	37
Emma Kemp	38
Robert Seal-Coon	38
Sam Sharp	39
Jonathan Smith	39
Anthony Williams	40
Florence Crawley	40

Bunwell CP School

Vaughan Williams	41
Ella Riley	41
Stewart Argo	42
Leah Wilson	42
Emily Hibberd	43
Matthew Eyre	44
Joe English	44
Jessica Harlow	45
Clare O'Connor	46

Caister-On-Sea Middle School

Crystal Foster	46
Lisa Wilkes	47
Leonie Battersby	47
Samuel Hubbard	48
Andrew Lees	48
Samantha Wedon	49
Jamie Brown	49
Kay Love	50
Kelly Lowen	50
Danielle Dawn Goodwin	51
Jodie Payne	52
Daniel Hurren	53
Kate Skidmore	53
Victoria Way	54
Hayley Brown	55
Adam Tolladay	55
Rebecca Shreeve	56
Lauren Payne	57
Kyle Hearney	58
Sam Greenland	58
Adam Brown	59
Louise Noon	59
Daniel Campbell	60
Robert Futter	60
Kim Holmes	61
Gary Etherington	61
Sarah Allard	62

Sara Crothers	62
Joanne Masterson	63
Brady King	63
Nicola Davey	64
Jemma Panther	64
Nichola Webb	65
Laura Simm	65
Jenna Kemp	66

Corpusty Primary School

Oliver Husar	66
Greg Brenchley	67
Sarah Thornton	67
Isobel Lacey	68
Jodie Bevan	68
Edward James Plumb	69
William Harrold	69
Hester	70
Catherine Perry-Warnes	70

Costessey Junior School

Kerry Scott	71
David Smy	71
Katie R Beauchamp	72
Jason Blunderfield	72
Thomas Chappell	73
Scott Frosdick	73
Stewart Harding	74
Elizabeth Metcalf	74
Sammy-Jo Roach	75
Hayley Motts	75
Adam Patterson	76
Lisa Raby	76
Sarah George	77
Helen Frankowski	77
Cheryl Heather	78
Claire Vincent	78
Ben Wright	79
Richard Moore	79
Victoria Dyson	80

Gary Mann	80
Neil Mickleburgh	81
Sarah Robinson	81
Lauren Brazier	82
Daryl Tooke	82
Andrew Gunby	83
Emma Louise Turner	83
Alex Edmonds	84
Sarah Rachael Staff	84
Carly Howes	85
Matthew Kevin Parfitt	86
Leon Raby	86
Rebecca Taylor	87
Christopher Elden	87
Kimberley Webster	88
Daniel Cornish	88
Helen Slipper	89
Judy Gardner	89
David Anderson	90
Samantha Heal	90
Kelly Sayers	91
Kayleigh Crocombe	91
Anne Carter	92
Thomas Ivor Lloyd	92

Grimston County Junior School

Katie Scott	93
Rachel Watkinson	93
Amy Dye	94
Hayley Sopp	94
Natalie Raines	95
Alexander Stride	95
Jenny Howard	95
Janey Knight	96
Lloyd Watson	96
Kerry Hollis	97
Sally Westrup	98
Rachel Darby	98
Oliver Rix	99

Daniel Roper	99
Patrick Kavanagh	100
Andrea Booth	100
Lewis Vanhinsbergh	101
Ellen Anderson	102

Mattishall Middle School

Emily Kreetzer	102
Katherine D Hamshaw	103
Helen Mark	103
Jenny Rhodes	104
Laura Cooke	105

Middleton VC Primary School

Keren Norman	105
Kathleen Lennox	106
Rosie Palmer	106
Rachel Everitt	107
Hayley George	107
Danny Goodson	108
Aimee Petch	108
Alice Brittain	109
Jack Dixon	109
David Norman	110
Paul Barrett	110
Toby Reeks	111
Danny Gardner	111

Mundesley Junior School

Nicola Craske	111
Katie Manders	112
Siân Grinsted	112
Claire Lowther	113
Jenna Rudram	113
Claire Glover	114
Marcus Granger	114

North Walsham County Junior School

Sam Gardner	115
Caroline Chapman	115
Edward Godden	116
Lucy Adams	117

Kimberley Prismall	117
Carla Tuddenham	118
Kelly Holt	118
Holly Maycock	119
Michael Popay	119
Liam Doyle	120
Heather Ward	120
Ben Thompson	121
Julie Reynolds	121
Kerri White	122
Roxanne Bird	123
Daniel Stolady	123
Patrick Burland	124
Angela Suckling	125
Helen Ogden	125

Notre Dame Prep School

Victoria Jones	126
Jenni Hayward	126
Keturah Eagling	127
Hamy Balakumar	127
Emma Louise Gale	128
Julia Patrick	129
Emily Clarke	129
Eloise Secker	130
Elizabeth Rhodes	131
Alexandra Gilbertson	132
Sophie Whitehead	132
Harriet Berridge	133
Alex Lingford	133
Gabrielle Kilian	134
Hayley Richards	135
Rachel Lane	135
Anna Rhodes	136
Vikki Ribbons	136
Joanna Norledge	137
Myrrhine Rhodes	138
Louise Ramsbottom	139
Molly Meachen	139

Faye Meredith	140
Yazmin Hussein Pettitt	140
Helen Faye Ewings	141
Alison Potter	141
Jeni Lentin	142
Sarah Ramjeet	142
Natalie Fish	143
Helen Victoria Tallent	144
Bethany Slaughter	144
Victoria Sutcliffe	145
Sophie J Donovan	146
Katherine Mills	147
Emma Brown	148

Old Catton Middle School

James Quantrell	148
David Wallace	149
Matthew Dye	149
Rebecca Mason	150
Ryan Dennis	150
Samuel Murray	151
Matthew Walkendine	151
Kirstie Gotts	152
Chris Kelly	152

Peterhouse Middle School

Louise Parker	153
Shani Hunt	153
Shane Darnell	153
Ashlee Thurgood	154
Freddie Hutchins	154
Luke Edwards	155

St Andrews CE VA Primary School, North Lopham

Susan Beales	155
Kate Horan	156
Victoria Knight	156
Thomas Lawrence	157
Vicky Oates	157
Richard West	157
Zaralee Sheldrake	158

Kelly Warnes	177
Scott Jonas	177
Paul Kitchen	178
Christopher Merkis	178
Emma K Squirrell	179
Glen Banham	179
Laura Smith	180
Elizabeth Stacey	180
Heidi Judd	181
Emily Wenham	181
Samantha Mason	182
Linzi Williams	182
Stewart McGovern	183
Thomas Bristo	183
Asa Skitterall	184
Lee Hammond	184
Harrison Puckett	185
Nina Ingram	185
Kelly Anderson	186
Siân Hughes	186
Nicholas Hodds	187
Brett Henderson	187
Ian Anjos	188
Toni Underwood	188
Dion Carr	189
Emma Barwick	189
Sara Moore	190

St Thomas More RC Middle School, Norwich

Luke Child	190
Peter Willson	191
Dominic Burke	191
Victoria Young	192
Suzanne Balcombe	193
Monica Mason	193
Joshua Kaye	194
Michael Kerridge	195
Aaron Bradley	195
Alexander Holland	196

	Shaun Hunton	196
	Joseph Clark	197
	Andrew Snowling	197
	Rachel Loughlin	198
	Stuart White	198
	Rosemary Bool	199
	Martin Race	199
	Juliet Goymer	200
	Patrick Maguire	200
	Jennifer Martin	201
	Jessica Anderton	202
	Thomas Arthurton	202
	Emily Joy	203
	Gemma Girdlestone	204
	Joseph Rutland	205
	Sophie Wright	205
	James Young	206
	Kay Field	207
	Mark Haydn	208
West Winch CP School		
	Kimberley Mclaren	208
	Sam Wells	209
	Nicola Symonds	209
Wormegay RC Primary School		
	Luke Allen	210
	Paul Harrod	210
	Edward Allen	211
	Luke Chopping	211
	Graham Britton	212
	Amanda Arndt	212
	Naomi Harrod	213
	Oliver Parker	213
	Rosie Moeser	214
	Robert Squires	214

ABERMORE

I like the sea,
It's bright and blue,
Whenever I go for a visit.
There are lots of fish,
Seagulls too,
And tons and tons of limpets.

Down on the seashore,
I can hear the waves
As I hunt for crabs and shells.
I search for fossils,
And maybe a stone,
Which I can take back home.

It's never crowded
And there's plenty of space,
To hear my echo around me.
The cliffs are high,
Almost reaching the sky,
And the clouds drift slowly above me.

Emilie Martin (10)

THE WINTER WOLF

The winter wolf has killed
The flowers of summer.
She is tearing the autumn
Leaves away from the trees
With her sharp white claws.
She has scared the birds away
With her cold ghostly howl.

The cold breath of the winter
Wolf has frozen the lake.
She has made the animals go
Into hiding with her dark
Growl.

The few animals that have
Remained have made a good meal
For the wolf.
They freeze, hungry in the cold

In spring the wolf has gone home
To look after her cubs
The flowers have come back from hiding
The birds have begun singing again.

Jack Davies (9) Aylsham Middle School

EPITAPH

Frazer McCloud

My parents thought I would be as skilful
as George Best,
As a boy I played *kick the can*,
I was goalie,
The mud splashed in my face as the ball
came towards me,
I hated it when that happened.
Then I married at 19.
I played for Manchester United, in the first
game still trying our team lost 5-0.
I knew then the truth,
I wasn't good enough.

Richard Crowther (11) Aylsham Middle School

SPIDERS

A spider is furry and tickly.
Big or small
Quick and alert.
They can be interesting
But some are dangerous.
Spiders are fast and cautious
And skilful.
Spiders have fangs
To kill insects
And they are blood thirsty.

Becky Hitchens (10) Aylsham Middle School

SNAILS IN THE CLASSROOM

Snails in the classroom,
Big and small.
Snails on paper leaving trails of silver,
And sly snails trying to escape.
Snails that are slow but have unique patterns.
Snails that are slimy but colourful too.
Snails that are small and pretty,
Snails that are big and bright.
Strong and stretchy snails,
Wet and shiny snails.
Snails are delicate.
Snails are fragile.
Snails have stripy curly shells.
Snails are peaceful and quiet.
Snails move cautiously and snails leave a glittering trail.
Yes snails are very interesting.

Sami Bainham (10) Aylsham Middle School

RAIN

The rain gushes in the gutter,
Beats against the window pane,
The thunder crashes down,
The windscreen wipers are on full,
They are squeaking whilst the water trickles down the
screen.

Claire Webster (10) Aylsham Middle School

CITY IN THE SUMMER

In hot and sticky streets,
People are moving slowly,
People hungry and thirsty,
Everyone tired and bored,
People try to find shade away
from the sticky heat,
Legs are aching, feet are dragging,
People struggle with trolleys and
baskets.

In hot and sticky streets,
Cars are rushing home.
Cars running out of petrol,
Hot drivers trapped in vehicles
Engines roaring, over-heating,
Bells ring and horns hoot,
Vehicles are driving up and down,
Buses struggling with their load,
The cars are gone and
everything is quiet.

Graham Reeve (9) Aylsham Middle School

THE SOUNDS OF THE CITY

I can hear the children shouting
And the cars racing by
The sirens of the police cars
The clubs are noisy like the cars
The ring of the church bells
The music of the buskers
And the hooting of the horns.

Ross Neumann (10) Aylsham Middle School

ON THE BEACH

I can hear the lapping of the waves
       on the shore,
I can hear my heart soft and slow,
I feel the soft breeze in my hair
I feel the sand under me,
I smell the salt hidden in the air
I smell sun cream
I touch the soft sand
I feel the sun touching me,

      The darkness draws in.

Helen Scott (10) Aylsham Middle School

SPOOKED

In the forest,
The movement of McThurson cries out
with pain from the war.
The sycamores sway as he moves from
north to south. In death he lives on
and on and on.

      The forest is in the war path,
      The path of the kids from
      town, but at night it is
      still. They have all been
      scared by McThurson
          Thurson
              Thurson
                  Thurson.

Chris Hardy (11) Aylsham Middle School

SPIDERS

Spiders are hairy
Eight eyes and eight legs
Jointed legs
Some are small
Some can kill
Tarantulas are dangerous
Some are fast
Spiders are blood thirsty.

Rachael Amis (9) Aylsham Middle School

NOT HIDING BUT SPYING

Nobody knew she was there.
But nobody heard her.
She was so far away,
She was not hiding but spying.

Wasn't she lucky the sweet
little girl.
Now she is running around.
Everyone thought she was energetic.
They said,

Oh, yes yes yes, she was.
Still nobody heard her.
As she was too far away.
But in the end she was not hiding
but spying.

Joanne Coxford (11) Aylsham Middle School

THE WOOD

In the gloomy old wood
The deep damp floor lay cold and still
Upon its surface lie muddy rustling leaves
The quiet air thick and spooky
The whole wood alive
Dark
Creepy
Wood
Misty
Wild
Place.

Through the droopy ivy
Lies a small dirty house
The walls covered in thick mud
Windows blocked with oak wood
Quiet as a mouse
Mysterious
Ghostly
Cottage
Cold
Hushed
Place.

Beth Grimsey (11) Aylsham Middle School

THE LITTLE COTTAGE

In the deep and creepy wood
The trees have spooky faces
The echoing of your voice
Through the misty leaves
Makes you hot then cold
Dense
Damp
Wood
Muddy
Mystifying
Place.

In the dark and dismal wood
Lies a cottage tucked away
Here stands a coffin
Where lies a ghost
Calling calling
I can't make out the sound but it seems like a name
Cold
Creepy
Cottage
Chilly
Quiet
Place.

Becky Foster (11) Aylsham Middle School

NOT SLEEPING BUT DYING

The old man lay upon the bed,
resting . . . you would have thought,
In fact to your disbelief,
he wasn't sleeping he was dying.

Elderly he was, he always loved his bed,
Now he's dead,
He was probably ill in the first place,
local folk said.

His sleep was too deep, with all those
nightmares . . .
but all along he wasn't sleeping but dying.

Kelly Garrard (11) Aylsham Middle School

RAIN

Rain beats upon the skylight.
Behind is dark cloudy night.
Will the rain never end?
Water runs down, splashing as
it goes.
The river swells muddy brown.
The rain is drumming, getting
harder.
Cars' headlights flash by,
Drops bounce off the road then
break and fall again.
Running down the gutter,
gurgling down the drain
People run for shelter.
Escaping from the rain.

Benedict Goodwin (10) Aylsham Middle School

NOT SLEEPING BUT DYING

Everybody heard him snoring, in his sleep
But nobody heard him dying.
Everybody saw him hobbling around.
But nobody knew his pain.

Everybody heard him snoring, in his sleep
But nobody heard him dying
They knew him as a young boy
They knew him as a man.
Always lazy and never working.

Everybody heard him snoring, in his sleep
But nobody heard him dying
Nobody knew why he died.
Must have been old age.
Nobody knew his pain because . . .

Everybody head him snoring, in his sleep
But nobody heard him dying.

Alice Eddy (11) Aylsham Middle School

NOT TALKING BUT SHOUTING

Nobody heard him shouting,
Everyone thought he was just talking
I was always too far away to know
What he was saying.

I feel sorry for him now, he liked to
Talk and now he can't.
They say he died of natural causes,
Now I know he wasn't talking he was
Shouting all his life.

Jennifer Bolas (11) Aylsham Middle School

11

THE SWEET SOUND OF SUMMER

In the summer you hear the
Bees buzzing around the
Flowers,
The birds sing their sweet songs
And the smells of apple trees
The white-throated sparrow
(Which goes) Phoebe, Phoebe
And the lovely smell of flowers.

Abigail Horton (10) Aylsham Middle School

THE SNOW IS WHITE

You can have fun too
And play lots of games.
Especially if you can throw
A snowball at your sister
In the winter you have lots of fun.
It makes your hands go very cold.
And the snow falls on house tops.
It's a surprise to me to see
All the snow.
Children have lots of fun in the snow.

Roy Pooley (10) Aylsham Middle School

THE WEB

The web is a delicate thing,
It sparkles in the daylight
And glistens at night.
The web is a home
To keep things safe.
One sticky thread can,
Supply food, and
Protect.

Lisa Kerrison (10) Aylsham Middle School

GOODBYE TO SUMMER

Summer has left, the
Dull winter has arrived,
People stay indoors
And sit by the fire.
All the animals hibernate
There's not a sound
The cold air makes you
Shiver inside.
People go out with woolly
Hats and scarves.
Snow may fall and make
Everything frosty and
Cold.

Victoria Lee (9) Aylsham Middle School

THE STORM

I was laying on my bed,
The clouds grew grey,
The sky grew white,
There was a storm brewing on,
The calm rain pattered on,
It grew harder,
Soon it was a storm,
The lightning was brighter,
The air grew cold,
The storm was here,
The thunder crashed,
The rain was firing,
It slowed down,
The storm was over.

James Scrivens (10) Aylsham Middle School

I KNOW IT'S DARK

I know it's dark and eerie
I know it's dark when the owls come out.
I know it's dark when the hedgehogs creep.
I know it's dark when the badger emerges.
I know it's dark when the fox pounces
I know it's dark when the moths flitter and flutter
I know it's dark when the bat squeaks from
a hollow tree.
I know it's dark when the deer come to drink
I know it's dark when the lady fireflies glow
in the moonlight.
I know it's dark when the birds go to sleep
on the branch of an old tree.

Clare Moll (9) Aylsham Middle School

HAPPINESS IS

Eating cold smooth ice-cream
Going on a sunny holiday
Playing fun football
Winning the lottery!

David Killingback (11) Aylsham Middle School

THE EAGLE

The
graceful eagle, gliding through the moonlit skies in front of a mountainous
background in Scotland. Preying on helpless rabbits and grouse,
ripping them up with its sharp talons and beak.
Mating time. Building a nest out of millions of twigs.
Finding a female to lay some eggs.
Hatching chicks need care and attention.
Getting old. Feeding requires a lot more effort. Death.
The graceful eagle, gliding through
the pearly
gates to make way
for a new generation.

Stephen Walker (11) Aylsham Middle School

A CLOUDY STORM

As I stand dripping
wet the wind blowing hard
against my face I see
a flash of light clashing
against each other.
The clouds look grey
and dark. They look like
they want to burst out
with rain. The leaves blowing
around like they are
being pushed by the wind.
The thunder is like a
big zig zag line.
It sounds like it is banging
big drums. The noises get
louder and louder until
it all ends in a loud
bang!

Lauren Robinson (11) Aylsham Middle School

HAPPINESS IS

Happiness is . . .
eating delicious ice-creams,
playing with friends,
going to the rec,
taking my dog to the woods.

Lisa Bix (10) Aylsham Middle School

16

MY TEDDY BEAR

One, standing in my cot with my
teddy bear,
Two, crawling around the house with
my teddy bear,
Three, falling around the park with
my teddy bear,
Four, walking around the garden with
my teddy bear,
Five, going to Gran's and eating food
with my teddy bear,
Six, having a party at home with my
teddy bear,
Seven, stuffing my face with my
teddy bear,
Eight, in bed sleeping with my tattered
teddy bear,
Nine, going to a football match and
jumping about with my teddy bear,
Ten, stuck in school doing work
without my teddy bear!

Tom Gardiner (10) Aylsham Middle School

HAPPINESS IS

Going out
People out of wheelchairs
Winning money
Having walks
Feeding pets
Getting things
Seeing people happy
Birthdays

Gareth Miles (11) Aylsham Middle School

SOMEBODY I KNOW

My best friend Kerry is very amusing.
My best friend Kerry has a habit of giggling
My best friend Kerry loves dogs, rabbits and puppies.
My best friend Kerry does not like crabs.
I will always be best friends with my best friend Kerry.

Stephanie Farrand (11) Aylsham Middle School

PEOPLE IN THE RAINFOREST

People who live in the rainforests don't
Envy us. They love their life
On the forest floor. They
Please themselves by dancing round the
Light of a fire with
Enough food for all.

In the rainforests there are
No shops. They eat all sorts, including

Termites! They eat
Honey, too. They
Even eat monkeys!

Rainforests
Are full of tribes
In small villages.
Not all are small,
For some are,
Oh, huge!
Rainforest people have
Ended up living in a lovely world.
Sitting in a forest is
Treasure for them.

Ryan Rust-Andrews (11) Aylsham Middle School

I KNOW IT'S DARK

I know it's dark when I see black everywhere
I know it's dark when I hear something run over the floor.
I know it's dark when I see you come up the stairs.
I know it's dark when I wake up at night
I know it's dark when I hear the owls go 'Coo coo.'
I know it's dark when the curtains are closed
I know it's dark when the moon is out
I know it's dark when the stars are out.

Craig Ellis (9) Aylsham Middle School

I KNOW IT'S DARK

I know it's dark when the owls come
out.
I know it's dark when the foxes come
out of their holes.
I know it's dark when the owls
go twit twoo.
I know it's dark when the birds go eee
eee eee.
I know it's dark when the badgers
come out.

Tom Southwell (9) Aylsham Middle School

THE SCARIEST WOOD

In the still wood
Dense trees are rustling,
Mysterious faces and quiet sounds
Damp and chilly leaves on the ground
The trees are alive, old and dark
The wood is
       murky
       dim
       and
       cold

In the wood
Is a dim dark cottage
Mystifying sounds drift from it
An old rotten axe by the door
The tool of a gloomy ghost
       cold
       damp
       place
       still
       echoing
       wood.

Leigham Moore (11) Aylsham Middle School

NOT HIDING BUT SPYING

Not hiding but spying
Good not to hide
I am spying on you
To see where you are
I can hear you
I can spy at night
And I can spy at
Midday and every way at night.

Michelle Dyjas : Aylsham Middle School

ALWAYS WINTER

It's never summer,
It's never spring,
The sky is always pale blue,
The snow is crunchy underfoot,
The trees are like mountains
            caving in on us,
The icicles are like sharp
            spears and swords.
Like transparent glass and
            precious diamonds,
The ponds are frozen,
The snowflakes are like
            floating stars,
The sun is fading low and red,
I am fed up with the winter
I am just fed up.

Rachel Sage (10) Aylsham Middle School

STORM AT SEA

A storm has overtaken us,
The lightning is zig-zagging,
The sky and clouds are grey,
The rain is pouring down,
Waves are crashing,
Water is splashing into the boat,
The crew are soaked,
It's getting foggy,
The boat is rocking from side to side,
It is blown off course,
Everyone is feeling cold and wet,
Looking forward to getting back,
To light the fire and get dry again.

Lisa Stearman (10) Aylsham Middle School

EVERLASTING WINTER

It's always winter, never warm,
Powdery snow everywhere in sight.
The cold air blown onto your face,
The sky is white, the sun is red,
Trees and bushes are covered in snow,
The icicles are like diamonds shining
          bright,
The low sun shines red on the trees,
The ponds are frozen over,
There is no sign of life anywhere,
It's still as rock,
The trees are like ghosts looming
          over you
It feels like winter will never end.

Scott Townsend (10) Aylsham Middle School

RAIN

Slowly, slowly,
Dripping on the window pane,
Trickling to the sill.

It's coming a little faster now,
Gushing in the gutter,
I wonder if it will spill.

It's drumming steadily on the roof,
The ground is shiny and wet,
The worms and snails are out.

It's coming a little slower now,
Just spitting on the pavement,
And tapping on the tiles.

Slowly, slowly,
Dripping on the window pane,
Soon it will have stopped.

Clare Walker (9) Aylsham Middle School

FOXES

A fox goes in his den
Catches prey for his vixen.
He moves swiftly and silently
Without making a sound,
And he caught a hen.

Tom Skoyles (11) Aylsham Middle School

THE STORMY DAY

It's going to be a stormy day today.
I do hope it won't rain.
Rain is wet, cold and splashy.
I look out of my bedroom window,
I see thunder and lightning.
Lightning lights up the sky.
The thunder banging every few minutes.

Lisa Rogers (11) Aylsham Middle School

ALWAYS WINTER

It's always winter, no life around.
The snow is crisp and powdery,
the land is cold and white.
No warm sun in the day.
Icicles hang like silver daggers,
spearing the caves and waterfalls
like transparent glass hanging in the
crisp air.
Water droplets like glittering diamonds,
fall from the icicles onto the snow-covered
ground.
Trees and bushes are covered in drifts
of heavy snow.
Frozen ponds and lakes are still as statues.
Snowflakes are like floating leaves in the
sky. The low, red sun is hanging in a pale blue
sky.

Simon Welfare (10) Aylsham Middle School

ONCE UPON A WINTER

Boots shuffling,
People slipping,
Scarves in use,
Cold air nipping.

Cars hidden,
Under slush,
Noses snivel,
Cold cheeks blush.

Heating on,
Houses white,
Chimneys cough,
Smoke light.

Bits of cloud,
Drop from sky,
Onto the ground,
And passers by.

Sun comes out,
Starts to rise,
Spring triumphant,
Winter dies.

Jeremy Wright (10) Aylsham Middle School

A WINTER LAND

The snow is just like powder
      glistening in the light,
The icicles are like ice spears,
The lakes are frozen,
The snow is like floating stars,
It seems it will never stop,
There is no sign of light or life
      in this winter land.

Lawrence Owen (9) Aylsham Middle School

WINTER RETURNS FOREVER

The snow is powdery white and glistens.
It covers every bit of land.
The snow glistens in the sunlight.
Icicles hang from the sky.
Flakes sprinkle down to the ground.
The icicles are like comets zooming from the sky.
They are like glass diamonds.
The sky is pale blue with clouds looping the sky.
The sun's power fades away and darkness returns.
Cold trees struggle for freedom from the biting snow.
Trees are like howling ghosts.
They scratch you when you walk through them.
They stick to you like a silky spider's web.
But animals dare not break the creepy silence.

Mark Fox (9) Aylsham Middle School

A WHEAT FIELD WITH CYPRESSES

The golden, blazing ripe wheat field
is at my feet,
The clouds are playing in the
wind.
Racing round and round
The air is calm,
The olive green cypresses are
bowing before the rich golden
wheat,
The poppies are gathered round
my feet,
The distant hills are green.

Beth Jex (9) Aylsham Middle School

A WINTER OF SNOW AND ICE

The snow is white and powdery,
Everything is white,
The sun's rays make the snow glisten,
The trees are all white,
The snow is falling from overhead,
The icicles are hanging from trees.
They are like transparent points of spears,
The trees and bushes are like ghosts,
The sky is blue,
But there is nothing else in sight.

Laura Davies (9) Aylsham Middle School

A WINTER-BOUND LAND

Powdery snow in a white glistening land,
Suspended between two shrubs a spider's web,
Looking so fragile and yet so strong,
Hanging like a veil of silk,
Each strand decorated with a pearl of dew,
Glistening in the cold light of a winter morning,
How carefully sewn and crafted,
In the middle a spider like a gem,
Still everywhere around,
No joy or celebrations,
Icicles hang from the trees like glass spears,
It's as if time has come to a dead end,
No change, just snow and trees,
The red sun shines cold over infinite snow,
A layer of mist hovers over the still ground
It is like night has taken over day,
A godless land,
No celebrations, no hope, just beauty.

Alice Lupton (10) Aylsham Middle School

A SPIDER'S WEB

How does the little spider make its silky web?
How does the little spider make its web so strong?
That is the question.
After a night's dew
The web is dressed in droplets of water
And to me a spider's web is a thing of beauty.

Ben Hepworth (10) Aylsham Middle School

28

A RAINBOW

Red, yellow, pink and green, orange and
        purple and blue,
It's God's promise to us and it's special
        to me,
The rainbow leaps across the sky impressing
        the world below
The colours of the rainbow loom over
        the tiny people as if it was a ruler
        above all rulers,
Yet disappearing as quickly as it
        comes.

Claire Foster (10) Aylsham Middle School

THE FROZEN LAND

White land glistening all around,
Powdery snow falling down,
Icicles transparent against the pale blue sky,
The animals sleep below the frozen ground,
Snowflakes like floating stars on the land,
The frozen pond is white and bleak.
The trees and bushes are weighed down with snow,
The sun is weak and pale red,
It's low, right near the ground,
Everything is still and cold in this frozen land.

Rebecca Botwright (10) Aylsham Middle School

WINTER IS COLD

It is winter
It is very cold
It is very white
There is snow outside
The snow is powdery
It glistens in the sun
The icicles are like diamonds
The snow drifts are like mountains
There is no-one around.

Robert Slaughter (9) Aylsham Middle School

A STORM AT SEA

The clouds loomed and threatened,
The lightning struck above,
Giant waves crashed down on the deck.
The crew were knocked over.
The rain stung us in our faces.
The wind howls all around.

Joe Houchen (10) Aylsham Middle School

A WINTER'S MORNING

The snow is powdery and crunches underfoot,
The snow dazzles as you walk past,
Icicles fall like iron gates,
Your surroundings are still,
Branches fall as the snow gathers on them,
The trees bend in arches,
Around you dark and shady trees gather,
On the horizon the sun gleams red,
The pale blue sky has little light in it,
The weak rays make the snow glow pink,
The sun has lost its pride
But something's creepy because . . .
The birds are quiet and won't sing,
There is no joy or laughter from the pub next door,
Everything is like stone statues,
There is no-one around,
It is freezing, silent and still.

Joe Riches (10) Aylsham Middle School

CAT

Perfectly balanced
She walks
Along the branch of a stooping tree.
Her eyes combing
The grass for any sign of movement
There's a rustle,
Then a pounce,
And she appears
With her unsuspecting prey
Limply dangling from her mouth.

Kate Creelman (10) Beeston Hall School

TERROR

It seemed I was walking for ages
The darkness of the room
Caught me, and
Swallowed me
I could not do anything.
I was as still as a rock,
The lights flung on,
My dad stood
Outside my room
I felt foolish.

Artem Kossenko (10) Beeston Hall School

BATTLE OF WITS

He moves his piece slowly,
Thinking.
His mind churning over endless nothings.
I take his piece.
His plan is lost, is victory gone,
For my enjoyment.
A smile creeps across my face and
Grandfather, lips pursed,
Thinks.

Tim Wilson (11) Beeston Hall School

A TURMOIL OF TRAMPS

Roaming, in the alleys
Sleeping in boxes
A penny for a loaf of stale bread.
Cold, discarded
Left to die in the streets.
Torn from warmth.
No love is shared with them,
Hated and ill treated
By the world.
Many pass by on the other side
There are no good Samaritans here.

Louise Watson (11) Beeston Hall School

VISION

He blazed through the sky
A yellow tipped beak,
The wings splashed with red
The tail blue as the mighty sea
A green no other colour could beat
And black for the talons
The white patch on the eyes reflects the sun,
As he flies away
The blinding colours fade into a dark streak.

David Abbott (10) Beeston Hall School

THE CLOUD PANSY

The cloud hides the sun
Peeping through a crack,
The five little clouds
Make one, in a beautiful clump.

The wild lion
Hides in the undergrowth
Prowling around, with its curious
Eyes looking at you
And growling through its short, but
Wild life.

The stalk is a ladder
Reaching up to the castle above
Once the ladder falls the
Pansy is no more.

When you pick a pansy,
Do not be scared,
It will not die,
It will grow and multiply.

Tom Clabburn (11) Beeston Hall School

CATHERINE WHEEL

The life of a pansy
Is very short,
It starts in a small
Bud protecting the
Delicate petals inside.
The flower is a baby,
Growing slowly,
Wrapped in its mother's
Gentle arms.
Waiting to be born.
The time has come,
Gently the bud releases
Her hold,
The blooming flower
Is like a Catherine wheel
Splashed with colour in
The centre.
Each petal is a butterfly,
Ready to wilt
And fly away.
Leaving their mother,
Hanging limply
From her square shaped stalk,
Beautiful in her
Own right, calling
Her children
Out of the dark.

Zoe Salton (11) Beeston Hall School

A SHORT LIFE

I suppose it gets bored
Just swinging to and fro,
Its only excitement
Is when it falls,
Down it comes,
Hurtling towards the soft spongy soil
Thud!
Is the noise it makes when it hits the ground.
Next, it appears in the fruit bowl,
Sitting peacefully,
Waiting
To be eaten
My mouth waters
As I pick it up
Rub, rub until it shines,
Crunch!
As my teeth pierce the skin,
The sweet and sour juice
Trickles down my throat
Until it's all gone.

Hannah Marsh (10) Beeston Hall School

ALONE

It seemed to me
That the dark
Brought things
With it, such as
Goblins and
Dragons,
I was always
Scared of
Them.

I would dread
Being left by
Myself, in the
House with
Those creatures.
The coats
Hanging up
Were the goblins.
The bench on the landing
Crouched
Like a dragon,
Asleep.

James Carter (10) Beeston Hall School

CLOWN

The clown circles the yellow ring,
His red nose is shining!
Those eyes, blue and white,
Lighten up his joyful face.
The huge pink shoes blunder on,
As the red mouth smiles.
The tiny green bow squirts water in his face.
And everybody laughs!

Emma Kemp (10) Beeston Hall School

ANTICIPATION

I watch as
It sways
Gently and slowly,
Threatening to fall
At the slightest touch
Of my hand.

The wind blows,
The apple falls,
Then I take a bite
Of the green, juicy skin.
Delicious.

Robert Seal-Coon (10) Beeston Hall School

FIRST DAY AT SCHOOL

There I was standing at the front of
My new school.
It was massive
Towering above me
I felt as if it was glaring at me.
We went in,
Everyone was chatting and laughing
But now with me.
I was so lonely.
Soon everyone had gone
Leaving me standing there.
I was wondering, would this ever end?

Sam Sharp (10) Beeston Hall School

MIRACLE

The pansy is like velvet
With a green twisted stalk
Different shades of green
The petals stick out randomly
The pansy with a yellow centre
Like an old withered man
Looking down at a small child
With an expression of love.

Jonathan Smith (10) Beeston Hall School

THE PANSY

The beautiful, different
Colours of purple, yellow and red
Are dancing under
The sunlight.
Tightly squeezed together in
A bunch, like a group of
Soldiers waiting to
Attack.
The pansy's little frilled
Face, looks like a pair of wings
As though he was meant to
Fly away
And at the end of summer
He lays his seeds and dies.
Ready for the whole process
To start all over
Again

Anthony Williams (10) Beeston Hall School

FASHION SHOW

The pansy is a ball gown
Swirling round and round,
With brilliant, vibrant colours,
Darting into each other, like a rainbow drifting in the clouds.

It glides back and forth, to and fro
Among the other beautiful, silky gowns.
But as the days go on
It turns tattered and worn
And floats gently to the ground.

Florence Crawley (11) Beeston Hall School

AT RUGBY

When I went
to rugby I was
okay I went
to have a game
I tried to tackle a
boy. I got the ball
and scored a try
I fell with a
bump. I felt dizzy
and went home.

Vaughan Williams (9) Bunwell CP School

SPRING IS HERE!

It's great!
Flowers blooming,
birds sing,
sun is out,
sky is blue,
bees are here,
trees are blossoming,
chicks are hatching,
ducks quacking,
lambs are born,
cows mooing,
chicks cheeping,
it's getting warm,
trees wave,
it's great!
Spring's here!

Ella Riley (8) Bunwell CP School

SPACE

I went up into space
I saw the bright stars
I thought it was ace
When I saw Mars

The stars are shining
I saw the moon's face
I thought space
Was a wonderful place

Stewart Argo (8) Bunwell CP School

SPACE

Through space I go
I see the earth
I see the sun
Oh it is fun,
I see Mars
I see the stars
I walk very slowly
Through the path of Mars
Space my favourite place
Back into the rocket I go
Past the sun past Mars
And the shining stars

Leah Wilson (8) Bunwell CP School

SPRING SO SWEET

Sun gazing over the hills

birds nesting
in the sun
spring has just begun
blossom on trees
falling
down
down
down
I watch the stream run
towards me
heads of flowers twinkling
in the sun
lambs bouncing over the hills
the grass waves
to me
I watch the sun fade
away behind
a cloud
then I know that
the day is out.

Emily Hibberd (8) Bunwell CP School

SWIMMING

When I am
>> under the water
I feel
>> it rushing into me
When I am
>> under the spray
I hear
>> it splashing above me
When I come
>> up from the water
I see
>> all the other people

Matthew Eyre (9) Bunwell CP School

SWIMMING

The water came
in my ears.
My head began to feel fizzy,
a gurgle sound came
as I went under.
I heard the ticking of my head.
When I came
up the sun
dazzled my eyes.

Joe English (9) Bunwell CP School

SPRING

Spring is
here again
the birds sing
the sun shines
Spring
the blossom
comes out
in summer with
leaves
Spring
clouds go
the sky gets
bluer
Spring
little goslings
are born
bees fly in
blue sky
yes spring is here

Jessica Harlow (8) Bunwell CP School

SPRING IS HERE!

Oh Spring is here!
Flowers growing,
trees blossoming,
bees are back,
birds singing.
Yes, Spring is here!

Oh Spring is here!
Sun's shining,
blue sky,
chicks hatching,
ducks quacking.
Yes, Spring is here!

Oh Spring is here!
Cows mooing,
horses neighing,
chicks cheeping,
lambs born.
Yes, Spring is here.

Clare O'Connor (9) Bunwell CP School

SPOOKS

Spooks are scary
Spooks are mad
Spooks are sometimes really sad
Spooks aren't funny
Spooks aren't nice
Spooks are terrible especially at night!

Crystal Foster (10) Caister-On-Sea Middle School

WINTER

Winter crawled
through the quiet house,
freezing windows silvery white,
turning the steaming ice to icy gold
though not a word was said.

Winter hurried,
through the empty town
freezing puddles and lakes
forming icicles, fingers poised magically changing all
around.

Lisa Wilkes (11) Caister-On-Sea Middle School

WINTER

Winter crept on,
through the Antarctic ocean,
waves crash against the rocks,
Hissing and prowling from the breeze,
it takes its last breath and not a word.

Winter crept,
on to the park
swings swaying with the breeze,
Nothing was to be heard,
until the day it never said a word.

Leonie Battersby (11) Caister-On-Sea Middle School

WINTER

Winter ran
through the silent forest,
freezing trees and plants,
killing insects and animals
as he went by.

Winter stepped
through the snowy city
freezing ponds and puddles

making fog and snow
and then moved slowly on.

Samuel Hubbard (11) Caister-On-Sea Middle School

WINTER

Winter crept
through the silent wood

freezing every insect, puddle and pond,
and then moved on.

Winter raced
through the forest
freezing twigs and lakes,
shaking branches,
crunching under people's feet.

Andrew Lees (12) Caister-On-Sea Middle School

SEASIDE HOLIDAY

I went to the beach on Monday,
I sat on a rock on Sunday,
I sat on the sand on Tuesday eating my
Ice-cream,
I swam in the sea on Wednesday
With the waves crashing on me,
I took my bucket and spade on Thursday
And played in the sand,
I took a bowl of water on Friday to
Collect some pretty shells for my
Collection,
I went again on Saturday to say bye bye
Because it was time to go.

Samantha Wedon (10) Caister-On-Sea Middle School

WINTER

Winter stumbled
Down the dark wood
Smashing down his victims
And burying the dead
Then moves on.

Winter fell
Into the cold water
Freezing it all with one blow
Then after catching his breath
He moves on.

Jamie Brown (11) Caister-On-Sea Middle School

TEDDY BEAR

Teddy bear,
Teddy bear,
I love my teddy bear.
He's big and fat
He's furry and he has spots
On him he has got a big nose.
He has got some hair.
He lies on my bed
Day and night.
I love my teddy bear,
I love him very much
He is lovely and soft to touch.

Kay Love (10) Caister-On-Sea Middle School

WINTER

Winter sneaked
upon us, the dark nights crept in
snow white, silent, twinkly and icy,
winter misty, unclear,
black and cold.

Winter quietly
comes around every year.
Freezing, blowing, cold and bustling.
Winter windy, whispering,
whistling flying by.

Kelly Lowen (11) Caister-On-Sea Middle School

50

THE MAGIC BOX

I will put in my box
        the sunset on a summer afternoon
the cold breeze from a winter night
        and a sister of my own age.

I will put in my box
        golden sand from a beach
animals of every kind
        and happiness for everyone.

I will put in the box
        as many books as I can read
all the stationery I will ever need
        and a huge rainbow for everyone to see

I will put in my box
        Boyzone and East 17
so they could sing.

I will also put in my box
        all the family that are dead
so we could be together again.

I will not put in my box
        terror of any kind
guns that will kill
        knives that will hurt

I will abseil down my box
        with all my friends and family
and we will all have Christmas
        together in my box.

Danielle Dawn Goodwin (11) Caister-On-Sea Middle School

THE MAGIC BOX

I will put in my box
A bright star which shines
And Christmas trees with lights.
A shepherd following a star.

I will put in my box
A snowman with a hat and scarf
Snow and people having snowball fights.
A pair of gloves and a scarf.

I will put in my box
A Christmas cake
A chocolate log
And a Christmas dinner.

I will put in my box
A dog's bark
And an alien from Mars
And all of the planets.

I will put in my box
The smell of flowers in springtime
The bright yellow sun hot in the sky.

I will put in my box
The cold wind blowing
A blizzard of snow.

Jodie Payne (11) Caister-On-Sea Middle School

A CLEAN PLACE

I will put in the box
A house full of money
A trip round the world
A hamburger, as big as me.

I will put in the box
A gigantic present
An Arsenal kit
And a scramble bike.

I will put in the box
A wish when I want one
A bright blue sea
And a big big house.

I will put in the box
A place without dirt in
A beach with no stones
And beds for homeless people.

Daniel Hurren (11) Caister-On-Sea Middle School

DOLPHINS

Dolphins are so lovely
They glide along the water like silk flowing in the wind.
Their call is like the call of the finest bird.
When you touch them it feels like you are touching glass
shimmering in the sun.

Kate Skidmore (9) Caister-On-Sea Middle School

MY MAGIC BOX

I will put in my box,
The first snowflake that falls to begin the year,
The first flower to grow in spring,
The glow of the warm summer sun,
The second leaf to fall to the ground.

I will put in my box,
The first meal of the day,
The first step outside,
The hot taste of my tea,
The warmness of the fire at the end of the day.

I will put in my box
The thankyou to be free,
The magic of a star,
The wish to fly,
The gift to stay young.

I have put in this box,
A year to remember,
My everyday gifts,
Things I have wished for,
And lots, lots more.

Victoria Way (11) Caister-On-Sea Middle School

MOONLIGHT

I went to bed early
I stayed up late
watching the stars nearly all night.
Suddenly the moon lit up
so bright that I could not see
it was the moonlight
shining on me trying
to tell me to sleep.
I said 'No' and
the light of the moon got
brighter then because the
moon was so bright I saw
a shadow saying sleep.

Hayley Brown (10) Caister-On-Sea Middle School

MY BEDROOM

What a mess my bedroom's in,
such a state that the late, great Einstein
wouldn't have been able to find his way around
the maze of clothes and shoes and penny chews!
I'm put in a daze when my mum says,
'Tidy this room!'
My heart sinks like a stone, I hear my head groan
as I try to find a place for *everything!*

Adam Tolladay 10) Caister-On-Sea Middle School

MAGIC BOX

I will put in the box
A large snowman with big round
eyes
Christmas trees with long pointed
leaves
A snowball fight with the winter
breeze.

I will put in my box
The smell of a Christmas cake
The taste of the turkey
And Santa's sack full of toys.

I will put in my box
Santa's eight reindeer pulling a sleigh
The crunch of the snow
And a bright star shining.

I will put in my box
A ray of sunshine
A star from the sky
And an alien from outer space.

I will put in my box
The movement of a ferry
The feel of the air at the top of
the Eiffel Tower.
The sound of a bus.

Rebecca Shreeve (11) Caister-On-Sea Middle School

CAT

It was early one morning when I saw her
Laying under a desk in a corner
She just lifted her head and opened one eye
Looked at me for a moment
Then laid back down again with the faintest of sighs
Was this a ghost?
I stood and stared in wonder
It was then I noticed its red and gold collar
Bringing back memories of bright summer days
Spent laughing in young carefree ways
Playing and chasing my cat Higgens all around
Until finally it would collapse under its favourite chair
Fall fast asleep for hours, and never stir
All of a sudden the cat had gone
Leaving an empty shadow cold as stone
Perhaps frightened by memories happy yet sad
Of the wonderful cat that I once had
But I still had a memory no-one could take away
The red and gold collar
At home in my drawer
A keepsake forever
So safe and secure.

Lauren Payne (9) Caister-On-Sea Middle School

WHERE'S WALLY?

Wacky weirdo
Handsome hero
Exciting quests
Red and white vest
Extraordinary cat
Stripey hat

Wizard whitebeards
Amazing trick
Laughing
Loudly
You'll need my magic stick

Kyle Hearney (9) Caister-On-Sea Middle School

BLACK

Black is the colour of a cool dark night.
Black is the coldest colour of all.
Black is the one that reminds you of death.
It reminds me of an abandoned graveyard on a dark cold night.
It reminds me of a witch's cat around the cauldron that bubbles
a spell.

Sam Greenland (10) Caister-On-Sea Middle School

WINTER

Winter skated
over the frozen lake.
Spraying chips of ice into the air.
Slipping and sliding.
Leaving a trail behind him.

Winter ran,
through the wide open meadows,
freezing each ear of corn.
Freezing the ground
and making each mouse go to sleep.

Adam Brown (11) Caister-On-Sea Middle School

DIFFERENT KINDS OF ANIMALS

I like cats and I like dogs
I like Guinea pigs, mice and frogs.
My brother likes wolves
My sister likes foals
My nan likes dolphins
My aunt likes moles.
My mum likes deer
My dad likes lizards
My friend likes polar bears that go out in blizzards.
It's nearly the end of this poem
I am very sad to say
If you can think of any more animals,
I'll write about them another day.

Louise Noon (9) Caister-On-Sea Middle School

THE FOUR SEASONS OF THE YEAR

Winter is cold and bitter,
Everyone stays inside in winter,
Winter's the coldest time of the year,
Winter's the time when Jack Frost's about.

Spring is when new life starts,
When the new flowers start to sprout,
Spring is when it gets really warm,
Spring's a good time of the year.

Summer's when it's the time of the year that's hottest,
When everyone's ready for a cheer,
Summer's the best time of the year,
Summer's the time when ice-lollies appear.

Autumn is when it starts to get cool,
So I wouldn't like to dive into a swimming pool,
Autumn is when animals gather their food,
Autumn's the best time of the year.

Daniel Campbell (9) Caister-On-Sea Middle School

THE SEASIDE

The waves go swish upon the stones, upon the shore,
The people gone, the sun goes down,
The beach is quiet once more,
Broken kites, lost balls and bats, smelly socks remain,
But then the waves come and wash the beach very
clean again.

Robert Futter (10) Caister-On-Sea Middle School

MY TEDDY

I like sleeping with my teddy
my teddy likes sleeping with me
when I cannot sleep
I cuddle him tight
then it is alright
I cannot sleep when teddy's not there
I never sleep without him
he sleeps at the side of my pillow each night
and when I turn out the light
he just sits there and stares at me.

Kim Holmes (10) Caister-On-Sea Middle School

CUP FINAL

It was a beautiful day.
On the pitch there was hay.
It was Arsenal against Chelsea.
Arsenal went 2 up
and had a chance of winning the cup.
But Ruud Gullit came on and scored
and the crowd roared.
The score was level at 2-2
but you wouldn't guess who
scored again? Super Ruud Gullit.
That made it 3-2 and Chelsea
won the cup and they were
all singing super super Ruud
Super Ruud Gullit.

Gary Etherington (10) Caister-On-Sea Middle School

THE CAT NEXT DOOR

The cat next door is big and fluffy.
The cat next door is big and round.
The cat next door is big and puffy.
His miaow is very loud.

The cat next door is very sweet.
The cat next door is very proud.
The cat next door would like a treat.
He gets told off 'cause he's so loud.

Sarah Allard (9) Caister-On-Sea Middle School

CARE FOR THE ENVIRONMENT

Care for the environment
it's up to you
forest, trees, and flowers too.

Oxygen and energy come out of these
rivers, seas, and oceans too
care for them it's up to you.

Birds bees animals too
care for them it's up to you.

Sara Crothers (10) Caister-On-Sea Middle School

HOW DO WE GET OUR NAMES

How do we get our names?
I know that our mums and
dads gave them to us but
how do we get our names?
Where do countries get their
names from. Some of them have
the strangest names like Thessaloniki
and Minsk. How do we get our names?
That's what I would like to know.

Joanne Masterson (10) Caister-On-Sea Middle School

THE FOREST

I am walking through the forest
with a tree next to me.

I am walking through the forest
look at you look at me.

I am walking through the forest
and I see some footprints.

I see the final footstep
it is a *rhino!*

Brady King (10) Caister-On-Sea Middle School

AT BEDTIME

At bedtime I shut my
eyes and go to sleep
then I dream about going
to the moon. I see strange
green aliens that try to
kill me. I travel through
the planets they're red, green,
blue and purple. I travel
through the stars which almost
blind me then I wake up.

Nicola Davey (9) Caister-On-Sea Middle School

THE DESERT SUN

The sun shimmers
in the hot desert;
Every day it shimmers
in the desert of the land;
It rises in the morning
then the sun dies in the evening;
The sun will never die forever
it will always stay.

Jemma Panther (9) Caister-On-Sea Middle School

MY DOG SANDY

My dog's name is Sandy,
She is golden like the sun
She sleeps with my dad because
She loves him the most.

My dog's name is Sandy,
She is very bouncy
Her coat is the colour of the
Sand.

My dog's name is Sandy,
She is fluffy and gold
My dog Sandy is very
Cute.
She licks your face when
You go in the door
Sandy, Sandy, you are the best
The best dog in the world.

Nichola Webb (10) Caister-On-Sea Middle School

THE BUTTERFLY

The butterfly hovers through the air
The silk on his wings like dust
Yellow, red and blue plus gold
Is this a dream?
In the wood the butterfly goes
He lands on a flower and sucks
Then flies off through the canopy.

Laura Simm (10) Caister-On-Sea Middle School

CAISTER BEACH

I stood on the lovely sand,
My bucket and spade in my hand.
The sun was like a golden ball,
Rising from the sea so tall.

I made a sandcastle, with a
Moat and a path.
With seaweed and stone and shells
Cut in half.
The day went too quickly,
It was soon time for tea.
But that night I dreamt of the
Sun and sea.

Jenna Kemp (10) Caister-On-Sea Middle School

SPRING

Lambs baa
Chicks tweet
Birds sing
Cows moo
Spring is here again.
Snowdrops rise from the ground
And daffodils bloom
Spring is here again.
It's hotter than winter
And buds are blooming again.

Oliver Husar (9) Corpusty Primary School

SPACESHIP

S pace is black
P lace is dark
A ir is not there
C ome on spaceman come on here
E aster is not there
S pace is night
H ow do they get up there?
I nk is in space Mum said it is not
P lace has no gravity in the dark.

Greg Brenchley (8) Corpusty Primary School

SPRING SPRING

Spring is good because birds sing.
Ladybirds go on green leaves.
Daisies come out and snowdrops drop from the
sky.
Ducks are swimming on the water.
The sun is shining.
We have May day in spring.
Bunnies hop and they hop hop everywhere.
We have Easter in spring.
We get chocolate eggs.
Butterflies fly.
The sun is hot like fun.
Spring spring spring. .
People skip.
Spring is lovely because it is fun.

Sarah Thornton (8) Corpusty Primary School

DELICATE WORLD

Delicate flowers growing on delicate tree.
All day long happily and green.
Delicate sheep losing their fur
As I was saying it could burn.
The smell was delicate and fresh.
The snowdrops are just going away.
Tadpoles have nearly come as frogs
And popped out of their eggs.

Isobel Lacey (8) Corpusty Primary School

SPRING

Spring's a happy time of year.
Blooming flowers ladybirds everywhere
People skipping and having fun.
Delicate snowdrops look beautiful
and birds singing beautiful songs.
Butterflies flying again
Bees buzzing and making yummy honey.
So beautiful you'll want to eat some.
And people playing in their
Swimming pool having lots of fun.

Jodie Bevan (8) Corpusty Primary School

SUMMER HARVEST

In the summer the country is yellow.
The fields are ready for harvest.
All the combines are out of the
barns ready for work.
The farmers are awake at 7.00 am out
in the beautiful field cutting the heads
off the wheat.
The spout comes out of the combine and
the tractor comes up and the combine
pours all the wheat into the trailer
and the tractor carts it away.
Lunch comes up and cups of drinks are
drank.
The afternoon sun is burning hot.
More and more dust gets into the
cab.
It's 7.00 pm 12 hours hard work
over farmers go home and get
a good night's sleep ready for
the next day.

Edward James Plumb (9) Corpusty Primary School

SPRING

S pring is fun in the hot sun
P retty daffodils are blooming
R efreshing showers are falling
I like spring
N othing but spring
G ood long days are on the way.

William Harrold (8) Corpusty Primary School

TREES

I love trees the way they make a noise when
the wind touches the leaves.
You can climb trees.
Hide behind when you're playing hide and seek.
You can use them for tree houses.
There's lots of different trees - oak trees, apples trees,
blossom trees, pine trees too.
I like trees they're my favourite thing.
Bark is rough leaves are soft.
Leaves are things you can play with in the autumn.
In the autumn the leaves are crunchy and brown.
When the wind blows they all fall down.

Hester (8) Corpusty Primary School

SPRING

Smell the sweet smell of blooming flowers like daffodils
and snowdrops
Hear the birds singing pretty songs and playing games.
Beautiful butterflies spread their wings and flower buds
come out once again.
The trees start blossoming, the bushes start flowering.
Lambs being born, bunnies playing.
Bees buzzing, frogs swimming, happy children, ducks swimming.
The sun starts shining, showers fall down.
Ladybirds crawl on green green leaves.
          Spring
is here at long long last.

Catherine Perry-Warnes (9) Corpusty Primary School

THE WATERFALL

Sliding gushing down down
down
Trickling trickling to the
ground
Gliding gliding through the
air
Falling falling down the
stair
Crashing splashing to the
ground
Until it calms calms right
down.

Kerry Scott (10) Costessey Junior School

OCEAN

The ocean is like an old wise man
Who is so expansive.
The ocean is so deep
And sombre
The old man sways back and forth
In his rocking chair
While people swim in him like a swimming pool

     The ocean grows like a plant
     And roots itself in rivers.

David Smy (10) Costessey Junior School

WATER WORLD

Water is sparkling and glittery,
Waves of an ocean blend together as
They rise upon the sandy shore.

An icy turn of a tap,
Makes water come out,
In icy glass tubes.
Its sparkling shiny skin goes wrinkly
Like an old woman's face.

Water swirls like a stream,
Rushing down waterfalls,
Sweeping the air with its whoosh!

Katie R Beauchamp (10) Costessey Junior School

A WATERFALL

A waterfall is big and powerful
A waterfall is smooth at times
But when it gets angry
It smashes and bashes
It slides everywhere.

It's sparkling and shining
It flows with such elegance and grace
At the bottom it crashes
The water goes everywhere
It shines like the sun.

Jason Blunderfield (10) Costessey Junior School

WATER

The water was surging
over the rocks as it rushed
through the countryside
swallowing anything in its
path.

On it rushed, faster and faster.
It got stronger and stronger
until . . .

Crash

Big rocks blocked the way
until a rock fell.

The water continued its journey
much slower sliding round
corners surging over rocks
until . . .
the
      sea.

Thomas Chappell (10) Costessey Junior School

POLLUTION

Pollution is bad,
Bad for our health,
Bad for our cities,
Bad for our wealth,
Nobody needs it,
Nobody cares,
Nobody sees it,
Nobody cares.

Scott Frosdick (11) Costessey Junior School

FOOD

Italy have their pizza,
America its fries,
France has got frog legs,
But we've got fish 'n' chips!

Mexico has chilli,
Sausages are German,
Scotland has the famous haggis,
But we've got fish 'n' chips!

Belgium has luscious chocolate,
Norway eats the fish,
India has lots of curry,
But we have fish 'n' chips!

Stewart Harding (11) Costessey Junior School

THE UNIVERSE

The universe is a big round ball,
Spinning round.
Hollow it looks,
We all imagine it's near us,

Far far away from us,
Far from the other planets,
It is so big,
Everybody admires the universe.

Elizabeth Metcalf (11) Costessey Junior School

HAMSTER FRED

I've got a hamster called Fred
He's a browny kind of red
He likes to munch on golden crunch
That's just my hamster Fred.
My hamster who's called Fred
Who's a browny sort of red
Who sleeps all day and is out of sight
And wakes and plays away all night.

Sammy-Jo Roach (11) Costessey Junior School

THE JUNGLE

Deep in the jungle,
There are animals everywhere,
Some big or small,
And some very tall.

There are also waterfalls,
High above the ground,
Where water flows,
And water grows,
Deep in the jungle.

Hayley Motts (11) Costessey Junior School

THE EARTH

The earth is a ball,
In which creatures crawl,
Searching for something to eat,
If they like plant or meat,
There is always something good to eat.

Big or small,
Short or tall,
Fat or round,
Flat as the ground.
Wonder how and wonder why,
Why do the birds fly in the sky?

The beast of the air,
And the beast of the ground,
Wasps are long and bees are round.
I wish I was a bird,
I know it sounds absurd.

Adam Patterson (11) Costessey Junior School

FOALS

Foals frolic
Over meadows
Amazing jumps
Leaping fillies
Showing off.

Lisa Raby (11) Costessey Junior School

SUMMER DAYS

We were going to the beach,
      but it was quite boring,
So I took out a pencil and a pad,
      and started a drawing.

I drew the yellow sand and the blue sea.
I drew the green grass and the shop selling tea.

I drew the trees' leaves ruffling and the
pink blossom puffing.

I drew the blue sky and the
fluffy white clouds going by.

I drew a flower with a bee,
and last of all I drew me.

And then I noticed a nice cool breeze,
while we were in the car going along with ease.

Sarah George (10) Costessey Junior School

PONY

Particular ponies love to roll
Oh how I love to watch them run and play.
Nothing can beat a thoroughbred
You wouldn't have a chance.

Helen Frankowski (11) Costessey Junior School

THEM OR US?

Dolphins glide through the ocean,
The water's clean and clear,
That's the way it used to be,
Before humans found their way here.

Monkeys swing through the trees,
Jumping and playing around,
That's the way it used to be,
Before humans cut trees down.

Tigers wander through the grass,
Beautiful and majestic cats,
That's the way it used to be,
Before humans wanted mats.

These animals will all die out,
In a battle they cannot fight,
That's the way it's going to be,
Unless humans play it right!

Cheryl Heather (11) Costessey Junior School

THE WITCH

T he witch is bad and mean.
H ear her making lots of horrid spells.
E verybody runs away from her.

W itches' claws sharp and pointed.
I nteresting smells come from her house
T ry the spells if you dare.
C rying noises from her hut.
H ear her shouting at the children she has caught.

Claire Vincent (10) Costessey Junior School

KING FROSTER

The icy snow falls
down around him.
High up the froster follows
him.
With a pale white face he
whistles to the wind.
His gentle white beard freezes
the heat.
He wrinkles the snow with
his wrinkled white skin.
He shatters the icicles
to diamonds.
As he settles the water
to light blue ice.
When summer comes around
the king froster dies to the
ground.

Ben Wright (11) Costessey Junior School

IN 1903

In 1903 there was a flea and he was
very lonely.

In 1904 he came to a door and knocked
on it very lightly.

The door was opened in 1904. But it was
too late for the flea.
Because he had been stamped on by me.

And that was the end of the flea.

Richard Moore (10) Costessey Junior School

THE CITY

The city is so noisy,
Shops everywhere.
Making everyone happy,
Washing and styling their hair.

There are so many shops,
I don't know which to choose,
Walking round and round
I'm going to blow a fuse.

Everyone is happy,
A smile on their face,
Smiling with laughter,
Walking a fast pace.

The city is so noisy,
Banging and crashing,
Music playing,
Windows smashing.

Victoria Dyson (11) Costessey Junior School

MY BOX

My box is made of silver sparkling shapes.
My box is one of the biggest things in
the universe.
A big piece of cheese the shape of a sphere

If I lived there I'd just fall to earth.
It's dark sometimes but the moon makes
it bright.

I'd hate to be there you'd hear all the
rockets go past.
If I was you I would stay on earth.

Gary Mann (10) Costessey Junior School

FANTASTIC FOOTBALL

Alan Shearer and Robbie Fowler
In all their grace,
Going for the top scorers' race.

Teddy Sheringham is the best,
He can beat all the rest.

Kevin Keegan has blown a fuse,
Because he has just lost to Man U.

Eric Cantona is number 1
For all the things that he has done.

Neil Mickleburgh (11) Costessey Junior School

PEOPLE

People as I stop and stare seem
to be everywhere.
I see people in the streets,
Or sometimes people buying sweets.
When they have eaten them,
They throw their wrappers down.
People kill dolphins, whales and seals.
They just leave them there.
All the smoke from all the cars
Pollutes the world right up to Mars.

Sarah Robinson (11) Costessey Junior School

WINTER WOMAN

She sweeps autumn out of the way
With her cold breath.
She rides a cloud like horse and glides
Through the wind.
She has pale white skin that matches
The frost.
Sparkly eyes that glitter like stars,
Silver lips that sparkle in the midnight
Moon.
With her horse she floats away,
Then settles like snow.
For winter is about to disappear
She will sleep until her time comes round
Again.

Lauren Brazier (11) Costessey Junior School

THE KOMODO FROG

The komodo frog has such a nasty bite
Everybody runs in fright
It has no friend because of his bite
It lives on an island in the shadows and the darkness
He comes out of his hiding place
His eyes like fire burning so bright
Licking his lips as he went on
Looking around for something to eat
If you see him run away
Go back inside.

Daryl Tooke (9) Costessey Junior School

THE SLIVER SLIMY SNAKE

The sliver slimey snake.
Who lives down in the creepy doorway.
It does not have any friends.
He is all by himself.
It looks very, very scary.
If you scare him he kills you.
It eats you.
It scares you.

Andrew Gunby (9) Costessey Junior School

THE LITTLE WHITE RABBIT

With his little white paws.
With his little white claws.

He runs through the snow
He sees a man with a gun,
He slows.

Bang goes the gun.
The man is fed
But now the little white rabbit is dead.

Emma Louise Turner (11) Costessey Junior School

IMPOSSIBLE DREAMS

In my dreams gold smells like money
money tastes like chocolate
chocolate sounds like snapping
snapping tastes like sharks.
In my dreams red is a big red sea but when I got
there it was a balloon so I pretended it was a
trampoline.
Once in my dream a football said stop kicking me
I've got a headache.
Once I tasted a rock it tasted like bubblegum
so I ate it all.

Alex Edmonds (11) Costessey Junior School

NOISE

I walk out my door,
Noise everywhere.
Next door's playing his drums,
Bang! Bang! Bang!
There's the cat,
Meow, meow, meow!
Here comes my nanny
With her dog!
Woof! Woof! Woof!
Hear the birds,
Tweet, tweet, tweet.
And that's the noise
In my *street!*

Sarah Rachael Staff (10) Costessey Junior School

THE FOX'S MEAL

Stalking around in the mist of the
morning,
Crunch goes the hard grass in the
frost.
Splish, splash, splosh goes the river
very slowly,
When anything walks through it.
No sound, it's stopped.
Flip, flop go the fishes in the
river.
Something's watching . . .
Splosh!
The fox missed the fish,
and went off.

Hop, hop, crunch, hop, goes the
rabbit on the frosty ground,
it stopped . . .
something is watching . . .
Crunch!
The fox got the rabbit and went
successfully home,
crunch, crunch, crunch, crunch, crunch.

Carly Howes (9) Costessey Junior School

THE LIGHTHOUSE

One day, a long long way away
stood a lighthouse with a sea monster
underneath it.
It saw the light and went
for a bite and there was no
lighthouse anymore.

Matthew Kevin Parfitt (10) Costessey Junior School

SUMMER LOLLY

S un shining down on the beach.
U nder the umbrella protecting you from the sun.
M en going for swims in the sea.
M um lying in the sun, trying to get brown.
E lsewhere, others in the ice-cream area.
R eally good at the beach.

L ovely lollies in the lolly van.
O thers going to the bar.
L ittle children playing bat and ball.
L icking lollies in your hands.
Y ou have to go now the beach is closed.

Leon Raby (8) Costessey Junior School

ICE-CREAM

Dripping ice-cream everywhere
Quick lick it, it's dripping
Hurry up and eat it
It's dripping down your sleeve.

Rebecca Taylor (8) Costessey Junior School

SUMMER LOLLY

S un shines like the stars
U p in the sky
M aking children blink their eyes
M aking the children cry
E ver, ever the sun shines
R eally so big but they don't know it

L ovely little lollies licked by lovely children
O n a lovely summer's day
L ollies are lovely
L ovely enough to eat
Y ummy yummy yum

Christopher Elden (8) Costessey Junior School

HORSES

My favourite hobby is horse riding
I go whenever I can,
I love to ride fast with the wind in my hair.
My favourite horse is called Sophie
She's always pleased to see me
Sometimes I take her carrots, and
Other times a sugar lump or three!
At the moment I can't ride her
Because she's a foal.
But I can't wait for the day when
I can have a horse of my very own.

Kimberley Webster (10) Costessey Junior School

SUMMER POEM

Summer is ultra hot.
Umbrellas called parasols keeping people cool.
Many people on the beach.
Many children in the heat
Energy in them.
Running down the sand.

Daniel Cornish (9) Costessey Junior School

WEATHER

Sunny days are brill.
Rainy days are boring days.
Showers are OK.

Sunny days are best,
Because you can play outside,
But sometimes too hot.

Rain is not so good.
Sometimes fun, sometimes not fun
Can't go out to play.

Showers are boring,
Still you have to go outside
Whether you want to or not.
Sunny days are brill
Rainy days are boring days
Showers are OK.

Helen Slipper (9) Costessey Junior School

LIFE BUOY

Life ring life ring quick quick quick.
Someone is drowning quick quick quick
Life ring life ring not a trick not a trick
Someone is drowning quick quick quick
Not a trick not a trick

Judy Gardner (9) Costessey Junior School

IF ONLY

If I could be a toucan a
toucan I would be,
Sitting up a tree eating berries,
as happy as can be,
All red, yellow, orange, black and
white,
I would love to be a toucan,
flying free across land and sea,
If I could be a toucan a
toucan I would be!

David Anderson (10) Costessey Junior School

THE BLACK CAT

As I look at the dark outside,
I see upon my wall,
A figure on black darkness,
Moving slowly then it jumps,
The shadow was tall and long,
First it moved slowly,
Then it moved fast,
Then it dashed across the grass,
Leaving nothing not even a trail,
Then I heard a squeal,
It came from outside,
From then on I didn't hear a sound.

Samantha Heal (10) Costessey Junior School

THE FARM

The other day I went to the park.
Next to the park was a farm.
All the animals got out of the
farmyard I chased them but
they were too fast.
They made loads of noises.
The pig went oink oink.
The horse went neigh neigh.
The donkey went eeyore eeyore.
The sheep went bah bah.
The chicken went cluck cluck.
The dog went woof woof.
The turkey went cock a doodle doo cock a doodle doo.

Kelly Sayers (10) Costessey Junior School

THE SEAMONSTER THAT POPPED OUT AT ME

Far far away in the ocean sea,
A giant seamonster stood in front of me.
He was slimy, he was tall, he was
much bigger than us all.
He ate my wellies, he ate my coat,
ate my food and my boat.
So he left me on my own,
swimming in the sea.
Soon he took a shine to me and
I was all gone.
Just remember
He was slimy he was tall he was
much bigger than us all.

Kayleigh Crocombe (10) Costessey Junior School

IF ONLY . . .

If I could be a rabbit,
I would jump around,
Jump jump jump!
Above the ground,
High jumps,
Low jumps,
Jumping all day long,
And when night comes,
I'd call back at the night,
And drum on the ground,
If only I could be a rabbit.

Anne Carter (10) Costessey Junior School

MY BLACK TROUSERS

On Saturday night I
Look at my black trousers
with a fright
Sometimes they look like a
cat or even a bat.
I go under the covers,
I don't know what to do
I cry myself to sleep
And wake up seeing . . .
A big, black, heap.

Thomas Ivor Lloyd (10) Costessey Junior School

STORM

Walking through the woods
Wheezy blackness brightened by the moon
The cackle of thunder stopping the bats hurling
Lightning covering the moon
A deep fiery pong of the wind creeping around,
And the heavy rain coming down
Deepness of black trapping you,
And the knife is stabbed.

Katie Scott (10) Grimston County Junior School

MY BABY SITTER

It's Monday night
Mum's doing Guides, Nic's gone too.
Dad's going to work,
Sarah the baby-sitter's coming.
Yippee!
I'm dithering about waiting for the doorbell to go.
Ding dong!
Yipee!
'Hi,' says Dad.
'Hi,' says Sarah.
Sarah takes off her really cool boots.
'I'd better be off,' says Dad.
'Bye,' says Sarah.
I say bye too.
Now for the fun!

Rachel Watkinson (10) Grimston County Junior School

SNOW

The snow is falling,
Clean and gleaming
Leaving an untouched blanket all around
It sounds crisp and crunchy as I walk along
The next day I look through the window
The snow has gone.

Amy Dye (10) Grimston County Junior School

SCARED

I could hear the creaking floorboards,
And the owl's hooting voice,
The thunder struck and I jumped,
I could hear the creaking floorboards,
And the ripple of a knife,
The boots squeaked and I blinked,
I could hear the creaking floorboards,
And the owl's hooting voice.

Hayley Sopp (10) Grimston County Junior School

THE CIRCUS

One day I went to the circus
To see the clowns and elephants
And the lions jumped out at me
One day I went to the circus
I bought some popcorn on the way
I sat near the back so the lions couldn't get me.

Natalie Raines (11) Grimston County Junior School

THE SKY

The smell of fresh air when the morning dawns,
The soft touch of the birds of the sky.
Wind gently blowing through the trees
The sweet sound of birds singing down below.
The sight of sparkling sunlight up above
Colours the bright, beautiful flowers down below.
A new day begins!

Alexander Stride (10) Grimston County Junior School

SNOW

Children playing in the glistening snow,
Making snowmen which will soon go,
Cold little fingers of children so small,
Cold little toes of adults so tall,
Snowflakes drifting from high to low,
Oh, I do love snow!

Jenny Howard (10) Grimston County Junior School

THE TRAFFIC JAM

The cars whistle by
Thick traffic stretches
For mile after mile.
Squeaking,
Creaking,
Coming to a stop!

Janey Knight (10) Grimston County Junior School

MURDER

He gets on my nerves.
It puts the temperature up.
I'd stab him if I could.
He gets on my nerves.
I would stab him in the heart.
The scream would go through my head.
He gets on my nerves.
It puts the temperature up.

Lloyd Watson (11) Grimston County Junior School

SCHOOL IS BORING

Sit down!
Stand up!
Don't talk!
Get to the back of the line!
Sarah, yes. Kerry, yes!
25 lines I must not shout out.
Go to maths.
Sit down be quiet!
Stop that Zara.
Corner Paul! Kerry,
Sorry Mrs Nell.
Stand up, go back Steven!
Don't do that Ellen,
Pick that up,
Be nice.
Playtime!
Shouting, screaming
I can't stand it!
English!
Dinner!
Work! Work! Work!
Home at last!

Kerry Hollis (11) Grimston County Junior School

SNOW

Sun shining bright,
The snow is glistening,
White and clean
First in the snow
Leaving footprints as I go.
Roads wet and slushy,
A raw, biting wind,
Icicles hanging
No more untouched snow,
The sky is cold and grey.

Sally Westrup (10) Grimston County Junior School

STARRY STARRY NIGHT 1889

As the moonlight beams through,
the darkest night.
Stars glinting down below.
I slowly walk through roses on a hill.
I stare down at the village sparkling
in the moonlight.
The wind twists and twirls around me.
Every star seems to glow
with pleasure and pride.
The moon is resting among hills and fields.

Rachel Darby (10) Grimston County Junior School

SOMEONE WALKING

I could hear someone walking
through the door it went swiftly
I hid under my bed shaking
I could hear someone walking
It was stampeding on the stairs like a
hammer hitting a nail
I saw the knife's shadow on the wall
I could hear someone walking
through the door it went swiftly.

Oliver Rix (11) Grimston County Junior School

MY CAT

I was my cat,
My cat that won,
That magnificent day, .
I ran on the track,
My heart beating so fast,
It felt so hard,
Like it was racing round my body,
We had won.

Daniel Roper (11) Grimston County Junior School

RUNOVER

The brakes were squealing
But it was still coming
I couldn't move
The brakes were squealing
My life rushed through my head
I was glued to the spot
The brakes were squealing
But it was still coming

Patrick Kavanagh (11) Grimston County Junior School

VAN GOGH'S EYES

The horse and cart trotted
along the bridge very quietly.
The water was calm and silent
until four rowing boats ruined
my view,
And the silence became the
sound of water.

Andrea Booth (11) Grimston County Junior School

THE GHOST SHIP

Floating,
Floating over a misty ocean.
Waves crashing,
I see a faint ghostly, misty, faded ship.
I've travelled back to the 15th century.
People working,
People praying.
A man stands at the front of the ship,
Old and skinny,
About to fall over,
Banging a big metal circular thing hanging on the ship's mast,
Bodies lay around it.
The ship begins to fade away into the distance,
Slowly disappearing,
Slowly.
I'm left again,
Over the mist.
Suddenly total darkness,
Everything quiet.
I wake up and find myself dreaming,
I live again.

Lewis Vanhinsbergh (11) Grimston County Junior School

MURDER AT FIRST SIGHT

I heard his money jiggling in his pocket
He was walking across the creaking floorboards.
His footsteps were coming closer
I heard his money jiggling in his pocket
He opened the door
Then he pulled the trigger
I heard his money jiggling in his pocket
He was walking across the creaking floorboards.

Ellen Anderson (10) Grimston County Junior School

YOUR FEAR

Your fear is your reality,
Enclosing you in its box.
Watching you with its glaring eyes,
Tripping, and trapping you.
You run into the darkness,
But you cannot escape.
It will always find you,
As you lay and wait.
You will never outrun it,
You can't use skill or wit.
Your fear is always with you,
'Cause it's mostly inside your head.

Emily Kreetzer (11) Mattishall Middle School

PENCIL TO PAPER

I was thinking, lying on my bed,
when a picture was forming inside my head,
so I put pencil to paper and started to draw,
all the things I had seen before.
I drew castles and seas,
people praying, knelt on their knees.
I drew pink clouds and skies,
birds up high.
I drew a valley with a river,
cold winds, shiver.
I drew ladies and men,
pink piglets in their pens.
I drew all of the things I've seen before,
until I couldn't draw anything more.

Katherine D Hamshaw (11) Mattishall Middle School

FIRE

A tall thin tongue of fire licks up from
the fire place.
Tiny devils dance and play in the flames,
Their strangely merry crackling as they
circle and chant.
Homeless children lay huddled in the
embers,
Their eyes wide and pleading.
Grey velvet ghosts drift silently through
the air,
Their soft fingers curl up to the sky and
vanish.

Helen Mark (11) Mattishall Middle School

JACK FROST

He creeps around day and night,
sly and silently.
His icy fingers are cold and pointed.
His heart is made of the coldest ice.
His eyes shine like green, green glass.
He has no friends because he chose to be a lonely boy.
But when he grew up the power he chose was
to rule this peaceful world.
His greedy face becomes the night,
while the rest of the world becomes the light.
He is locked up in the gloom,
whilst the children of this world dance and
laugh, sing and play.
When the north wind blows that's when he
will strike;
he will not lose a battle.
He will go on trying until he does conquer the world.
The victim is the world because it cannot defend itself.
He has upon his greedy face a grin which
stretches from ear to ear.
His nose is pointed,
small and thin.
His bony structure stands behind your windowpane.
However much you try you cannot win,
he will never go away.
He's the character you will never forget.
Jack Frost is his name.

Jenny Rhodes (11) Mattishall Middle School

AUTUMN

Autumn is near,
The nights are getting colder.
The sky gets darker as night time falls,
As the silvery moon rises,
The barn owl calls.
You can hear the leaves crackling,
As Jack Frost comes out to play,
Freezing everything he touches,
Dancing the night away.
The leaves are changing colour,
From green to golden brown.
You can hear them whistling in the wind
As they tactfully fall to the ground.
The squirrels are collecting nuts,
Ready for hibernation,
The birds are lined up on the wires,
Preparing for migration.
In the light of the moon,
The cobwebs appear,
Shining like crystals,
So delicate and clear.

Laura Cooke (11) Mattishall Middle School

FIRE!

F rightening and hot,
I gnites anything in its path.
R oaring down towards you,
E mbers burning very hot.

Keren Norman (11) Middleton VC Primary School

SYLLABLE POEM - FLOWERS

Long
Lasting
Very nice
Orange flowers
They are beautiful.
Flowers dying
Very sad
More to
Come

Kathleen Lennox (10) Middleton VC Primary School

SYLLABLE POEM - GYMKHANA TIME

Jump
Dressage
Cross country
Gymkhana games
It's all fun today
Now it is time
I can't wait
I *won*!
Great

Rosie Palmer (10) Middleton VC Primary School

SYLLABLE POEM - DINNER TIME

Shout!
Mum says
Dinner time
Lovely food today
I like chicken
Delicious
Yum yum
Great!

Rachel Everitt (11) Middleton VC Primary School

THE MAGIC JEWELLERY BOX

Inside my magic jewellery box
is a secret.
It might be . . .

A gorgeous ring shining,
An ugly witch casting,
A cunning star whistling,
A beautiful girl singing,
A glistening pen hovering,
A pretty crystal glowing,
A bright sun sparkling,
A clever book telling.

I don't know.
The secret is locked
Safe inside.

Hayley George (10) Middleton VC Primary School

THE MAGIC FOREST

Inside the magic forest
is a secret.
It might be . . .

A bald eagle hovering,
a small owl gliding,
a small kestrel flying,
a long snake slithering,
a fast cheetah running.

I don't know.
The secret is locked
safe inside.

Danny Goodson (10) Middleton VC Primary School

SYLLABLE POEM - RAIN

Rain's
Pouring
Thunder roars
Bonfire is out.
Wind is blowing strong
Lightning flashes.
Pot smashes
Dogs bark
Woof!

Aimee Petch (10) Middleton VC Primary School

THE MAGIC BOX

Inside my magic box
Is a secret.
It might be . . .

A grey horse neighing,
a magic tree glowing,
a hunted tiger prowling,
a curious giraffe watching,
a muddy elephant wallowing,
a blue whale swimming,
a slow river sparkling,
a happy panda laughing.

I don't know .
The secret is locked
Safe inside.

Alice Brittain (10) Middleton VC Primary School

SYLLABLE POEM - EAGLE

Fly
Eagle
Fly away
From your eyrie
Soar upon the wind
Glide eagle glide
Smooth and swift
Landing
Now.

Jack Dixon (11) Middleton VC Primary School

SYLLABLE POEM - SLEEP

Close
Your eyes
You don't want
To go to sleep
Don't lay down to rest
Or have a dream
Go on - sleep
Sleep please
Snore!

David Norman (9) Middleton VC Primary School

SYLLABLE POEM

Kites
rising
going up
wind gets stronger
wind's taking control
wind's dying down
coming down
look out
crash!

Paul Barrett (11) Middleton VC Primary School

CATS

C reeping
A gile
T errifying
S linky!

Toby Reeks (11) Middleton VC Primary School

FIRE

F ire is hot
I t burns.
R acing along,
E ating everything in its path.

Danny Gardner (10) Middleton VC Primary School

STARS

Stars stars twinkle
all night.
twinkling twinkling
ever so bright.

Shine through my window
ever so bright,
high high up
in the sky.

Nicola Craske (11) Mundesley Junior School

UNIVERSE

Stars in the sky,
That twinkle so high.
Big bright stars that are so,
Far from me.

I look further to
The planets,
Mars has green people,
That sing like screeching things.
Saturn rolls around the stars,
While the sun beams down,
Onto the flowers.

Katie Manders (11) Mundesley Junior School

THE HORROR MOVIE

A box of popcorn in my hands,
Screaming groaning clanking pans.
Horror movies are such fun,
They are watched by everyone.

A big man with a gun
A murderer on the run.

Big slimy monsters sliding everywhere,
Crawling, creeping up the stair.
Bang on the head, oh my word,
He's dead!

Horror movies are the best,
Are you going to put them
To the test?

Siân Grinsted (10) Mundesley Junior School

THE DENTIST

In the dentist,
On the chair,
Looking around everywhere
Where's my mum?
Where's my dad?
If they were here I would be glad,
What's that noise,
Oh I am scared,
How I wish that someone cared,
I looked around and there he was
Standing there with a big drill,
Ouch that hurt,
Oh I'm glad it's all over now.

Claire Lowther (11) Mundesley Junior School

IN THE SWIMMING POOL

In the swimming pool
I splash all around
Water going everywhere
I go under water
And go swimming under there.

After a while my
Hands go wrinkly and
I look like an old woman
I love swimming
Until it's time to get out.

Jenna Rudram (11) Mundesley Junior School

THE DENTIST

I go in and sit on the chair,
How I wish my parents were there.

Then I see the big mean drill,
Or is it something that
Will kill.

I want to scream,
I want to shout,
But there isn't anyone about,
Except the dentist behind me.

Oh oh, now I see the nurse,
Then behind her something worse.
The thing that I always dread,
the
needle!

Claire Glover (11) Mundesley Junior School

SCHOOL DINNERS

Yummy, yucky,
Slushy, sludgy,
Rubber cheese,
Mushy peas,
These describe
School Dinners.

Slop slop goes the gravy,
The cook's gone crazy,
Always leaving the dinner,
Want to run back home,
Eat a tomato sandwich,
Then start the afternoon
           full!

Marcus Granger (10) Mundesley Junior School

114

MY LONG LOST WIFE

As I am growing old each day,
I think of my long lost wife called Kay.
As we sat by the fire we talked and talked,
About the ground and fields we'd covered and walked.
Until one day, In the month of May,
We were in a field of sheep and hay,
But then I saw her fall to the ground,
She managed to cry 'I love you' out loud,
She never said anymore,
She laid at peace on the floor.

Sam Gardner (10) North Walsham County Junior School

THE WORD WITH NO VOWELS

This word has no vowels.
It has a world of its own.
It has chucked the vowel out
And left the letters alone.
The word is unknown.
It has no
Power.
The vowels have the power.
The word is
No use.
It has no meaning.
It is useless.

Caroline Chapman (9) North Walsham County Junior School

THE FORGOTTEN TOY

When I was Edward's best toy,
Used every day,
Down the garden path,
Always the fastest racer,
With a bonnet like polished
Brass and red roses,
In the summer,
My driver Edward was really so proud of me,
So why did he leave me,
Pack me away,
In an old dusty box,
With lots of spiders and sniffing rats,
I thought he liked me,
I thought I was cared for,
I liked him so much,
Especially when patted,
Even though it hurt,
Now I'm all dusty, all alone,
Apart from a filthy old
Battered clock.
Going tick-tock,
I wish he was back,
Playing with me,
All I can hear is tick-tock,
Tick-tock,   Tick-tock,
Tick-tock,   Tick-tock, tick,
Tick-tock.

Edward Godden (9) North Walsham County Junior School

FLOWERS ARE LIVING

Every time you pick a flower it screams in dismay.
Hates being taken away from its friends and its home.
It just gets picked and put in a vase.
No consideration,
Although it shares a vase with two other flowers,
They are horrible to him.
His light purple coloured,
Wonderful petals,
Are fading.
Drooping rapidly.
He's dying.
Life's not worth living.

Lucy Adams (10) North Walsham County Junior School

MY BROTHER'S A DEMON

My infant brother is a demon,
With a spotty face,
Big red roaring eyes like fire.
His bedroom's like a bottomless pit,
With little demon friends running around.
When *my* friends come round to play,
He scares them,
Makes them cry.
He scribbles over walls,
Books.
Chucks his food around.
Makes everything a mess.
But when he's in bed,
He's all cuddly and sweet.

Kimberley Prismall (10) North Walsham County Junior School

THE ELEPHANT

The elephant is like a rumbling earthquake.
Stomping down on the ground.
It's almost like he's saying
Go, leave me alone.
Massive, grey and bold.
Like a big dustbin can.
He sounds like a powerful voice
Shouting down a tube.
He's almost a giant, a tumbling, clashing,
Bashing, bad-tempered gorilla.
He moves like someone dropping a brick down
In slow motion.
Feels like a silky night-shirt.
He stands out.
He would tower above a crowd.

Carla Tuddenham (9) North Walsham County Junior School

SNOW AND MORE SNOW

Snow falls gently white cold and feathery.
Frozen icicles hang.
Light in the morning, dull in the afternoon.
Very deep thick ice, thick snow.
Very slippery as you go.
My nose goes red, I feel numb.
I shiver as I walk.
I throw snowballs.
See snowmen that have been built.
Snow comes down feeling soft like feathers.
It dries up and gets cold as winter can be.

Kelly Holt (10) North Walsham County Junior School

FIRE BELL

There it was
Perched on a high part of the wall.
The most scariest thing alive
The fire bell.
All of the class were afraid
Especially me.
The way it screamed
Terrifying.
Quickly run outside
Get into a line.
Ring aling aling
There it goes again
Red is the colour
The colour of fire.
But I suppose I will get used to it
As the years go by.
Ahhhhhhh

Holly Maycock (9) North Walsham County Junior School

SUN

Sun rise fun starts
Light shines
Sunglasses out
Good sunshine
Sun dies
Cold comes
Fun stops for winter
Until next time

Michael Popay (10) North Walsham County Junior School

IT

It hides amongst the shadows
with its creepy crawly eyes,
eyes not filled with wonder,
only with despise.

It watches from a distance
seeing beauty, it has none,
and slowly starts to hate
everything and everyone.

Slithering and sliding,
it does not make a sound.
The only way to know it's there
a grey trail on the ground.

It is small and slimy,
its ugliness offends.
No-one has ever loved it.
It has no need of friends.

Liam Doyle (11) North Walsham County Junior School

ICE-CREAM MAD!

My name is Kerry,
I love strawberry
It's better when it's melted.
The creamy cream,
The icy ice,
It's heaven when we're wilted.
The mint inside the mint choc chip soaks my tongue and teeth to ease,
And when mum gets the ice-cream out I say 'Can I have some?
Please, please, please!'

Heather Ward (9) North Walsham County Junior School

DEBIT

The title sums it up doesn't it?
Most of the teachers have a blue fit,
Their hair covers their twisting horns,
My teacher must be a monster,
Her horrible purple tangly hair,
Her drooling fangs,
Her stinking cheesy breath,
Her bloodshot beady eyes,
Her debit's like her bite,
Debit Debit Debit,
Is what she says all day,
But I'm acting like an angel?
Help me God I pray,
But the worst thing is . . .
They keep you in all play,
I wish they weren't all monsters
I'd have a happy day.

Ben Thompson (10) North Walsham County Junior School

THE BEACH

Crashing waves on the sand
Stones and pebbles hit the ground
Jellyfish starfish birds and crabs
Rough and gentle sea
Smelly fish, shining stones

Grey blue green and more colours
The sky is all sorts of colours too
Beautiful sky calm sea
Noisy sky rough sea

Julie Reynolds (10) North Walsham County Junior School

121

AS DAYS GO BY . . .

As days go by,
You must never lie,
Nor disobey,
Never get in the way,
Eat what's on your plate
And choose a decent mate
Go to bed on time,
Always make your poems rhyme,
Always be polite,
Never bite,
Never punch,
Have good manners when out to lunch,
Never kick,
Never take the mick,
Never disagree,
Never take the key,
Do your best at school,
Always play it cool,
Wipe your feet,
Never have a second sweet,
Never be tough,
Never be rough,
Don't watch too much TV,
If you do all these you see,
Your parents will be happy!

Kerri White (11) North Walsham County Junior School

WHY, OH WHY

Why, oh why do I see,
Something as wonderful as a tree?

A tree can give us many things,
Like shelter, shade, birds that sing.

Trees can give us fruit and flowers,
Which could amuse a child for hours.

And yet then man is such a clown,
To cut these glorious trees down!

So why, oh why do I see,
Something as wonderful as a tree?

Roxanne Bird (11) North Walsham County Junior School

SNOW

Snow soft and delicate and very gentle,
Cold as ice, but very fluffy deeper and deeper it gets
As each and every snowflake touched the ground.
Jagged like star snowflakes are, very delicate and gentle.

Snow storms, blizzards causing chaos everywhere.
As I walk in a blizzard my face goes cold and
My fingers numb,
Snow can be horrible as well as gentle and kind.

Daniel Stolady (10) North Walsham County Junior School

I AM THE WIND

I sleep then at the crack of dawn
I howl and moan and groan
I wake
I let out a puff of wind
Leaves take off
Slowly glide back to the ground
I blast dustbin lids everywhere
The rubbish from inside is scattered in the garden
When I blow hard
I sometimes see kites
Flying high in the air
I sit and gaze at the kites for hours.
I love to play tricks on people
I make a lovely cool breeze
And the lifting of big fluffy wigs and hats
Makes me laugh
I whistle
I scream
I echo
I sing
And be bad
And especially unforgiving
I twist and turn round trees
Zig zag round trees
Twist and turn violently
I howl like a wolf weakly
I am public weather villain number 1
I terrorise people then run away
I hope to come back another day

Patrick Burland (9) North Walsham County Junior School

THE WINTER

We get in the car.
We skid on the road,
Fog in the air
Trees with no leaves
Rain thumping on the window
My ears are cold
Everywhere white looks very nice
I go out to play
Build a snowman
Have snowball fights
I love playing in the snow

Angela Suckling (9) North Walsham County Junior School

SNOW

I woke up one morning,
Got out of bed.
I pulled the curtains.
This is what I saw
A layer of white snow
With freshly laid footprints
Leading to the garden shed.
The branches on the trees were
Swaying this way and that.
The grey clouds towering over
The village below, my cat was running
To shelter, to feed on a freshly killed
Mouse.

Helen Ogden (9) North Walsham County Junior School

SPRING

Animals born
Birds nest
Flowers bloom
Spring is here.

Lambs dance
Rabbits hop
Chicks hatch
Spring is here.

Birds feed
Fluffy chicks
Trees grow
Spring is here.

Birds sing
Ducklings swim
Sunny days
Spring is here.

Victoria Jones (9) Notre Dame Prep School

FEET

There are many kinds of feet
Some are big, and some are sweet
Wide and narrow
Webbed and clawed
To fit any pair of shoes you can afford
To dance and swim
To hop and run
Oh they can be so much fun!

Jenni Hayward (9) Notre Dame Prep School

AUTUMN

Lovely jams
Scarlet leaves
Juicy fruits
Autumn is here!

Shorter days
Smoky bonfires
Falling acorns
Autumn is here!

Shiny conkers
Tasty nuts
Beautiful hip
Autumn is here!

Bouncy squirrels
Dead flowers
Cold wind
Autumn is here!

Keturah Eagling (8) Notre Dame Prep School

THE MONSTER

There's a monster under my bed,
And I can't get him out of my head.
I've tried and I've tried,
But I'm really wide eyed.
I just can't get him out of my head.

There's a monster under my bed,
I've seen him in books I have read.
He's ugly and scary,
Gruesome and hairy,
I just can't get him out of my head.

Hamy Balakumar (9) Notre Dame Prep School

COLD

Today I woke up,
And I couldn't
Get out of bed,
I was so cold.

Later on when I was dressed,
Ready to go to school,
I put on a scarf and hat,
And then I went out.

I was really cold,
It was snowing,
And the wind was,
Blowing and blowing.

I was freezing now,
Even when I was in the car,
You can't hide from the cold,
It's everywhere in the world.

It was hailing now,
I ran into school,
As quick as I could,
I was freezing.

And after school,
I went home to bed,
And to sleep,
Now I am warm in bed.

Emma Louise Gale (9) Notre Dame Prep School

128

WINTER'S END

No wearing hats and gloves.
No having dark cold nights.
No having frost on cars.
Winter has gone.

No chimneys smoking.
No hot water bottles.
No feeling cold.
Winter has gone!

No having power cuts.
No playing in the snow.
No building snowmen,
Spring is here!

Julia Patrick (8) Notre Dame Prep School

BOOKS

I read lots of books at night,
When mum and dad are tucked up tight,
I read and read and read and read,
And then succeed to read some more,
While there you'll find beside my bed,
More books are waiting to be read.

Much later, when my mum and dad,
Come in to see if I'm asleep,
They see me reading books galore,
Some thrown across the bedroom floor,
And even stacked against the door,
All my books are in a heap
I just don't want to go to sleep.

Emily Clarke (8) Notre Dame Prep School

SPRING

Baby lambs
Chicks hatching
Daffodils blowing
Butterflies flying
Spring is coming

Sunny days
Lighter nights
Winter ending
School holidays
Spring is here

Rabbits jumping
Bluebells swaying
People playing
Swallows flying
Spring is here

Nesting birds
Cracking eggs
Fluffy chicks
Hard work
Spring is here

Eloise Secker (8) Notre Dame Prep School

WEATHER

Weather is funny,
It's unpredictable,
Like a hopping bunny,
Going this way and that.

Weather is hot,
It is strange,
It's all we've got,
It's confusing.

Weather is cold,
It is weird,
It nips the old
And the young as well.

Weather is cloudy,
It is sometimes scary,
It blows very loudly,
It is angry.

Weather is funny,
It's unpredictable,
It blows away your money
To the edges of the earth.

Elizabeth Rhodes (9) Notre Dame Prep School

SPRING

Hatching chicks
Fluffy chicks
Golden chicks
Growing chicks

New flowers
Coloured flowers
Pretty flowers
Lovely flowers

Blue sky
White clouds
Yellow sun
Spring is coming.

Alexandra Gilbertson (8) Notre Dame Prep School

THE DIZZY DUCK

One day while I was feeling rather lucky,
I walked down the road and came across a ducky
He waddled around on his little webbed feet,
Looking around for a play mate to meet.

He splashed around a puddle
Chasing his feathery tail around,
But he looked rather in a muddle,
As his tail kept going round and round.

When finally he stopped spinning round
He fell in a heap sprawled out on the ground,
I picked him up and stood him straight,
Then watched him stagger out of the gate.

Sophie Whitehead (11) Notre Dame Prep School

SUMMER

The sun shines down so hot each day
It's summer so we can go out to play
The garden is bright and warm
I feel sleepy I give a yawn.

The beach is busy with people today
The sea is cool and relaxing compared to the sun's rays
And climbing on rocks and exploring rock pools
The breeze blows it is fresh and cool.

The fields are green the water is clean
A picnic is fun in the summer sun
Cake, and sandwiches and orange juice
Fruit and cheese and chocolate moose.

But I like summer with lots of sun
And games, and fun,
So when the day is really over
I sit and daydream how nice it's been.

Harriet Berridge (11) Notre Dame Prep School

ANIMALS

Animals come in many different sizes
Some are big
Some are small
Some you cannot see at all.

Some animals creep around in light
Some are only seen at night
Some animals the human eye
Has not even seen.

Alex Lingford (10) Notre Dame Prep School

WATER, WATER EVERYWHERE!

We're using water everyday,
All the time in every way.
Brushing our teeth,
Washing our hands,
Everyone's using it all over the land
Water, water everywhere!

We're always drinking
Swimming in it
Playing and splashing around in it.
Hear the waves crashing, what a loud sound,
But the colours are so magnificent
Water, water all around!

Water in the ponds,
Water in the lakes,
Water in the seas
All being destroyed by pollution
So stop it please
Water, water everywhere!

Water drops shine in the light
And look like crystals
They roll off the leaves
And fall on the grass
Please look after if, it's everywhere!

Gabrielle Kilian (10) Notre Dame Prep School

WASTED WATER

Water!
Without it we would die
So here is a poem
Just to make you try to
Stop wasting water

Think of all the poor people
Out there in the desert
Working in the hot, hot sun
You might say it's dumb
But just for five pence
Someone could have a drink
Instead you go and waste it
Why can't you see
That more than one child dies a day
Either from pollution or starvation
So I'm writing this poem to say
Please stop wasting water

Hayley Richards (11) Notre Dame Prep School

LIFE

Water gives life
Without water
We would not be here
The frogs would not be here
To lay their eggs
The birds would not be here
To feed her young
The people who live far away
Might get a cup of water a day
We are lucky today because . . .
A cloud is near.

Rachel Lane (11) Notre Dame Prep School

135

FIREWORKS

Six o'clock off we go,
get your hat and scarf.
To the park off we go,
this is going to be fun!

At the park, we get the food,
popcorn, hot-dogs and sweets.
Then we go to the ring,
so we don't lose our seats.

Then we hear the speaker go
'Please don't go in the ring.'
Then the fireworks start,
this is a brilliant show.

Flashing lights all around,
red, orange and blue.
Big bang what a sound
I wish I had one too.

Anna Rhodes (11) Notre Dame Prep School

DOLPHINS

Dolphins splish,
Dolphins splash,
Dolphins glide,
Dolphins dash,
Dolphins dive,
Dolphins cry for one another when they're unhappy,
They glide through the water with one big whoosh,
They jump up and down, and swim round and round,
Dolphins are quiet and sometimes rest,
I have to admit dolphins are the best.

Vikki Ribbons (11) Notre Dame Prep School

HOW DOES RAIN COME DOWN?

It drops down from the sky.
That's for sure.
But I want to know,
How?

Perhaps there is a giant
Way up there in the sky
He must be sitting on a cloud
I think he's hurt,
That's what makes him cry
The tears fall on the streets and towns.
No! A giant would be too heavy for a cloud.
He would fall down to the ground!

Then maybe it is God,
Maybe when he is angry
He throws buckets of water,
Down at the earth.
But I am not sure, you see,
I am told the air is taking the water
Secretly to the sky
Then when a cloud gets heavy
The rain comes down,
But I want to know, why?
I wonder what do you think?

Joanna Norledge (11) Notre Dame Prep School

FULL OF WATER

In the garden
in a hole
there is a pond
full of water

There are lots of pond plants
such as
lilies, reeds and pond leaves
There are animals
such as
frogs, tadpoles, snails and bugs

In the pond
it's full of life
so don't disturb it.
Look at the frog's big round eyes
staring at you

The fish are swimming
all around
watching for some food
to come along

The evening draws near
and it's getting very cold
all the animals have gone to bed
and so have I.

Myrrhine Rhodes (10) Notre Dame Prep School

SUMMER

The summer sun shining down,
There's no need for my dressing gown.
The blue sky up above,
Oh I wish I was a silk white dove
To fly up there in the sky.

In the warmth I'd play,
Right in the depth of May.
I sit and make a daisy chain,
And I'm glad it does not rain
Oh I love the summer sun.

All the little animals are hot,
But I'm really not.
The cheerful summer sun,
Oh what a lot of fun.
Summer!

Louise Ramsbottom (11) Notre Dame Prep School

WHY

I want to know why birds fly?
And why some children cry?
I want to know why camels have humps?
And why when I fall I get bumps?

I want to know why the sky's so blue?
And why do cows go moo?
I want to know why stars shine so bright?
And why is there day and night?

Why?

Molly Meachen (10) Notre Dame Prep School

CATS

Black cats, white cats,
Orange brown and tabby cats,
Long fur, short fur,
Soft groomed and shiny fur,
Cats that scratch,
Cats that don't,
Cats that purr,
Cats that cry,
Some that look you in the eye,
Wild cats tame cats,
Lazy, learned loyal cats,
Strong cats, weak cats,
Old, young and new cats,
All do the same thing,
And that's *sleep*!

Faye Meredith (11) Notre Dame Prep School

SPRING IS . . .

Spring is flowers, bright and gay,
Spring is the sunshine that shines in May,
Spring is the birds flying high in the sky,
Spring is watching the ducks go by.

Spring is long lazy days,
Spring is the fields full of maize;
Spring is barbecues in your back garden,
And spring is everything I can imagine.

Yazmin Hussein Pettitt (10) Notre Dame Prep School

FROGS

Some people think they're slimey
Some people think they're wet
Some people just don't like them
But I think they're great.

Some are small
Some are large
But it doesn't matter to me
Because I just think they're great.

I go down to the pond on a
Very sunny day
And pick them up to help them
To get out of the way,
The bikes ride round the pond
Too close to the edge.

Helen Faye Ewings (10) Notre Dame Prep School

NATURE

Nature lies there under my eyes,
Amphibians, birds and insects,
The turtle glides with menacing tides,
Under rocks, creatures lie
Red ants, beetles and spiders
Endless nature

Alison Potter (9) Notre Dame Prep School

ANIMAL STAMPEDE

Lots of animals in the world
Some have 4 legs some have 2
Some have none at all
Some even have 42!

Some walk
Some slither
Some stamp
Some swim in rivers and seas.

Some are domesticated
Others are wild
Like a prowling lion
Or a puppy playing around

We like our animals so don't kill them.

Jeni Lentin (10) Notre Dame Prep School

COOKING

If you're not good at cooking,
Can't bake or fry,
This is something you can try.
3 large rotten eggs
1000 hairy spider legs
Some bat wings
And some creepy crawly things.
Squash tadpoles on toast
And rat roast.
Some mouldy leaves
And several dirty handkerchiefs.
This poem might give you a twitch
You've guessed it I'm a witch.

Sarah Ramjeet (9) Notre Dame Prep School

HAMSTER

Sweet and furry
Cute and cuddly
He burrows through his bedding
Stuffs his cheek pouches full of food
And scurries back to bed
Zzzzzzzz!

He goes for a midnight snack
Or in our time a midday snack
He goes back to bed
Zzzzzzzz!

Yawn!
He hears his name being called
He sleepily goes to the edge of his cage
He finds a treat
Munch! Yum! Munch!
He goes back to bed
Zzzzzzzz!

Yawn!
Wake up time
He scratches at his cage
He wants to go for a run
Now he is out
And running about
Now he is back in his cage
Zzzzzzzz!
Then the day starts over again.

Natalie Fish (9) Notre Dame Prep School

FLOWERS

The winter has gone,
So has the snow
And now in the gardens
Spring flowers start to grow.

Daffodils, primroses and
Crocuses too
Bring colours in shades of
White, yellow and blue.

Next is the summer
And daisy chains to make,
There's roses and petunias
Then autumn leaves are left to rake.
'What pretty patterns they make.'

I like all the flowers that God made for me
But I love the white snowdrops
They are a real joy to see.

Helen Victoria Tallent (10) Notre Dame Prep School

THE YEAR

There are four seasons in a year,
Summer, autumn,, winter,
Spring is here.
The weather changes all the time
Hail, snow, rain and shine

Spring is the beginning of the year,
Then summer the hottest season is here.
Autumn, all the leaves fall off the trees,
Winter, now everything starts to freeze

Winter seems long and harsh,
Then spring creeps up from the marsh.
Summer time for fun and ice cream,
Autumn, in the mist the sun loses its gleam.

Bethany Slaughter (9) Notre Dame Prep School

FISH

They swim in rivers, ponds and seas,
And dart round corners under willow trees.
They have scales to make them glide,
Through rivers as they dive.

Sea fish sometimes change their colour,
And bigger fish are much fuller.
Exotic fish are very bright,
Some like the dark, some like the light.

River fish like pike and trout,
Fishermen usually catch them out.
Carp and salmon swim very fast,
Until the fishermen catch them at last.

Pond fish like minnow and char,
Cannot swim very far.
Roaches big and very stout,
I hope that they will not die out.

Victoria Sutcliffe (10) Notre Dame Prep School

SNOW

Snow, snow is exciting,
Snow, snow is inviting,
Come out to play,
The snow won't stay.

Let's make a snowman,
that will need
A scarf and hat,
Perhaps he'll fly me away,
As long as I get back
today.

Skating in the cold breezy air
Snowflakes falling on my
hair.
Slipping, sliding, snowball fighting.

Snow, snow is exciting,
Snow, snow is inviting,
Come out to play,
The snow won't stay.
Snow, snow
don't go away.

Sophie J Donovan (9) Notre Dame Prep School

ANIMAL SEASONS

Swallows swirling round and round;
Peeping mice are in the barn;
Rabbits looking for a burrow;
Insects start flying about;
Nests are being made by birds;
Gobbling geese waddling round.

Some little birds are flying around;
Under a leaf there is a slug;
Mammals bringing up their young;
Mini-beasts are being annoying;
Eagles flying in the thermals;
Robbing magpies stealing all sorts.

Animals getting ready to hibernate;
Under leaves the squirrel's nuts are;
Trees are losing all their leaves;
Up in the sky the swallows gather;
Moles are driving gardeners crazy;
Nightingales cease to sing.

Woolly lambs are now young ewes;
In the hedges the animals are;
Nothing seems to move;
Tortoises are asleep;
Everything is bare;
Resting till the spring.

Katherine Mills (9) Notre Dame Prep School

THE EAGLE

The eagle flies
Up in the sky
Over cliffs and streams
It flies wherever it wants
The wind pushing its feathers
The sun shining on its back
Over open country it flies by
It sees all beautiful things
It flies happily and freely
How I wish I could fly with it

The eagle's not free now
It is hunted by man
It should be able to fly far away
From the people who want to kill it
I don't think it's fair
What has it done to us
Man can be so cruel

Emma Brown (10) Notre Dame Prep School

FIRE

Little flames and big flames fighting
High smoke rising higher and higher
When I sit in a chair
I can hear the flames piling up
It sounds like rattling tins
The fire gets hotter and hotter
Sparks flying up the chimney
They are orange and red and purple
The flames are big and pointy
I feel good when I look at the flaming fire

James Quantrell (9) Old Catton Middle School

FIRE FLAMES

Space rockets shooting out.
The engine on fire everywhere.
Colours are bright red, yellow and orange.
The fire is spitting in disgrace.
And in its place are wood and ash.
The smoke's like a dragon with a bad cough.
Sparks spitting everywhere.
Burning your red face,
Swirling and winding as the flames go upwards.
Hurts your eyes if you get too close.
It's like an oven with the gas on
As the wood burns ash begins to come.
It reminds me of a dog begging for more
Wood and a steam-roller with its smoke.

David Wallace (8) Old Catton Middle School

THE FIERY FLAMES

The fiery flames licking the wood as it burns.
Flying in the air like a beanstalk growing.
Out the fire like bats flying in the air
A dragon blowing fire.
Flames flying very high.
Like a house on fire.
Yellow, orange and red.
Hot, big flames fly in the air very high.

Matthew Dye (9) Old Catton Middle School

THE WALK IN THE DARK

I feel as if I am being watched as I walk through the dark wood.
I can feel the cold on my face and feel frightened but I walk on.
I can't see a thing. I trip and nearly walk into a bush but I still walk on.
The trees look like witches with long fingers that grab me.
I think I will get lost and never see my mum again but I feel
Great as I walk into the house.
Some people weren't scared but I don't want to go again.

Rebecca Mason (9) Old Catton Middle School

IN THE DARK

When we went outside,
It was very, very dark and cold,
I felt a bit scared when I
Thought we were going in the graveyard,
I felt my cold cheeks,
I heard cars going by and footsteps
From the person in front,
I heard the wind rustling,
And people talking,
I heard the noise of
Leaves that we were
Standing on,
As soon as I saw the light
Of the house,
I was really glad.

Ryan Dennis (9) Old Catton Middle School

THE NIGHT WALK

When I walked through the wood
I felt so cold
My back was frozen as I followed the person in front
As I came through the wood I saw everything was different
As we came back I remembered the route to the centre
In the middle of the walk we changed direction and turned around

Samuel Murray (9) Old Catton Middle School

THE NIGHT WALK

It was awesome as we walked through
The forest, as the ground seemed to move,
And I was walking all over the place.
It was bumpy and lumpy in the field
And the ground seemed to break away like
Plastic.
The stars moved with us and
The north star glowed like a cinder of
Coal, but white.
The trees were scrawny like spikey hands
They seemed burning with light.
As we walked past the river I saw the sparkle
Of the stars and the river flowing.
The church was a rectangle tall and steep
In the blackness.
It got lighter, I like the dark it's
Great!

Matthew Walkendine (9) Old Catton Middle School

BURNING FLAMES

I like sitting near the fire
Shining in the dark.
It burns the rubbish.
It seems like snakes
Winding up and hissing.
It is very warm if you
Put your face near it.
Don't get too close
Or you could burn.

Kirstie Gotts (8) Old Catton Middle School

THE SUN

Sun come out, out to play.
To brighten up the day,.
Then when it's night time,
You can go and sleep behind
The moon.
Then in the morning you can
Brighten up the day.

Chris Kelly (9) Peterhouse Middle School

HAVE FUN

S wimming is fun
W e do lengths
I n the pool
M y mum is happy because I am going swimming
M e and my friends are happy because we are going swimming
I t is summertime in May
N ever dive in the swimming pool
G going down the swimming pool every day

Louise Parker (9) Peterhouse Middle School

THE MOUSE AT NIGHT

If you walk down the street at night
You will see a bright, bright light.
In that bright light you see
Is a mouse as quite as can be.
If you were to walk to it
Change your mind until the mouse is out of sight.

Shani Hunt (8) Peterhouse Middle School

SKELETONS

Skeletons in a bed
Skeletons up a tree
Skeletons crawling up my knee
Coming to get me,
Skeletons on my head
Skeletons on my bed
Skeletons try to scare me when
I am already dead.

Shane Darnell (9) Peterhouse Middle School

THE SUNSHINE

S un is like a fireball,
U nder the ground in the winter is where the badger sleeps,
N ever get sunburn always put a T-shirt on.
S un is the hottest thing near the earth.
H appy people go down the beach for a walk.
I n summer there is no room down the beach.
N o dogs are allowed down the beach.
E verybody eats down the beach in summer.

Ashlee Thurgood (9) Peterhouse Middle School

MY FANTASY LAND

My fantasy land is where unicorns play,
And Pegasus flies in the sky by day,
And the dragons come out at night to play,
And fly around the moon.

There are rivers that run round the valleys,
Rivers that run crystal clear,
Where the River God and his daughters live,
His daughters, ever so dear.

All of these sites are as true as can be,
In my world, my world of fantasy,
And all of the people are there to greet me,
When I visit my fantasy land.

Freddie Hutchins (9) Peterhouse Middle School

OUR WORLD

We live on the world.
Our lives depend on it.
Rulers of the world should treat it carefully.
Look after the world and,
Don't spoil it.
Because if we do then eventually
We'll all die and humans will be extinct.

Luke Edwards (8) Peterhouse Middle School

LOOKING BACK

As I walk slowly
In and out of the trees.
Frightened.
I feel someone watching me.
The twigs below my feet - snap!
Behind me
Like an echo?
Snap!

Susan Beales (11) St Andrews CE VA Primary School, North Lopham

FOG

Fog is a beautiful lady
Dancing through the fields.
Breathing her frosty breath
Hanging drops on the spider webs
Making a jewelled necklace.
Dancing.
      Dancing.
            Dancing.

Kate Horan (11) St Andrews CE VA Primary School, North Lopham

FOG MAN

An old man dressed in rags
He wraps you up
In a cold damp blanket.
Fog,
Makes the webs of spiders
Glimmer and sparkle
With drops
Like diamonds on a chain.
Fog,
That old man
Dressed in rags
Has given his diamonds away
How sad he is. How sad.

Victoria Knight (9) St Andrews CE VA Primary School, North Lopham

WIND

The wind is so cold
I can't keep still
My teeth are clattering
Against my jaw
It must be time
For school to start
Please oh please
Just open the door

Thomas Lawrence (9) St Andrews CE VA Primary School, North Lopham

MIST CAT

Mist is like a grey cat
Purring round you
Making you shiver
He lets you out of his grasp
As he creeps slowly away.

Vicky Oates (9) St Andrews CE VA Primary School, North Lopham

AEROPLANES

Aeroplanes darting across
The sky like swallows.
Swooping in the sun.
But sometimes they are
Like hawks in the sky.
Silver and dangerous
Like lightning.

Richard West (11) St Andrews CE VA Primary School, North Lopham

FIRE LIGHT

Feel
It wrap round you.
Reach across the room.
Easing about me.

Like blankets.
I'm safe now but
Getting
Hotter! The fire is not
Tame.

Zaralee Sheldrake (9) St Andrews CE VA Primary School, North Lopham

MY FRIEND CONKER

Conker peeps out at me
From the long grass.
The crack in its prickly case
Seems to be smiling at me.
I kneel down.
He says 'What's your name?'
I say 'Kathryn.'

Kathryn West (8) St Andrews CE VA Primary School, North Lopham

BULLYING

There's a girl at school
She says I'm ugly, stupid,
And my teeth are horrible.
I wonder if I should tell?
Or does she do it
Because she is sad?
If I get her into trouble
I feel I am just as bad.

Emily Goddard (10) St Andrews CE VA Primary School, North Lopham

TADPOLE

I am a little tadpole
Very dull am I
I only swim around all
day
I can't even fly
But this will change
And I will be a big and
handsome frog
I will leap about and
catch flies
I will live a very exciting
life.

Anita Baker (8) St Johns CP School, Hoveton

THE FROG CONVERSATION

I never had these long legs before.
I started in some eggs.
Did it happen overnight?
Isn't it a nasty fright?
What can I be?
Please tell me.
Where has my tail gone?
I feel very alone.
Why have I got flat feet?
I wish with someone I would meet.
I gaze at myself in the pond,
The likeness of it I am not fond.
I wish I was a tadpole again.

Pierre Le Moignan (7) St Johns CP School, Hoveton

THE FROG

I am a piece of frog
spawn
Floating in a pond
I will hatch into a tadpole
Eating all the pond weed
I am getting bigger every
day
Soon I have grown back
legs
Six days later I have
grown front legs
Soon I am a frog with
webbed feet and big eyes
I can hop now and go on
land and eat flies.

Zac Bowman (7) St Johns CP School, Hoveton

A FROG

A frog I am in brown and
yellow.
I hope you look at me again.
I lay eggs and I am waiting.
Under a tree to jump.
Into a river.

Kayleigh Bond (8) St Johns CP School, Hoveton

TADPOLE

A tadpole am I,
As others go by,
When I grow to be a frog,
I'll be jumping on a log,
I remember being in spawn,
That was were I was born,
I am a tadpole black and tiny,
I have eyes which are shiny,
Now I have two hind legs,
When I am a frog I am going
To have eggs,
Now I am a frog,
I can't stop jumping on my log.

Andrew Lake (8) St Johns CP School, Hoveton

LITTLE FROG

I am a frog green and
yellow
Who jumps about
From lilypad to lilypad
And I am as happy
As a frog can be.

As I sit under a bush
I watch the little insects
Flying by my nose
I smile at them
And say
'You are in a hurry to day.'

Amber Bowyer (8) St Johns CP School, Hoveton

I AM A HAPPY FROG

I am a happy little frog
As happy as can be
I am a frog slimy and wet
In the summer I lazily lie
in the river.
Sometimes I sit under a
bush waiting for an insect
so I can snap it up.

Daniel Bull (8) St Johns CP School, Hoveton

THE FISH IN THE FISH TANK

It's boring swimming round and round,
with nothing to do without a sound.
I've got nowhere to go and nothing to do,
I just swim around being lonely too.
I always hear the cats at night,
they always give me a big fright.
I need a much bigger space,
than to stay in this horrid place.
I always wanted to be free,
and swim in the big sea.
I miss my old friend Frank,
he's probably in a luxurious tank.
But round and round I swim,
looking at my tank with nothing in.

Eleanor Dawson (9) St Johns CP School, Hoveton

THE TADPOLE

I am a tadpole all black and
tiny,
I have eyes which are shiny,
I am beginning to get back
legs,
At the moment my mum is
laying eggs,
Yesterday she laid seven,
But today she laid eleven,
In six weeks time I will be a
frog,
Sitting on a brown wooden
log.

Tim Mortimer (8) St Johns CP School, Hoveton

WINTER

Cold and icy,
      Freezing all day,
Wind blowing in my eyes,
      Ice-caps all around,
Ice-skating down the lane,
      Snowballs thrown,
Snow falling from the sky,
      Ice-caps over plants,
Echoes far away,
      I like winter
      Do you?

Jade Ellis (9) St Nicholas' Middle School, Great Yarmouth

SPIDERS

Little spiders, big spiders,
making a web.
They go in your bedroom,
and climb in your bed.
Every spider
I have seen,
they all have hairy legs.
They knit a web
nearly every day.

Nikki Almond (9) St Nicholas' Middle School, Great Yarmouth

WINTER

Cold and icy,
As light as glass,
Very deep, very cold,
Icicles everywhere with snowmen around,
Slush is nice but has ice.

Cold and icy,
Really misty in the air but very spooky,
Children playing in the snow,
Saying No! No! No!
Then it's time to go to bed Oh! No!

In the morning, it's time for school,
My feet crunch on the way,
When I get there I am late,
When it is play time the snow flows,
Snow, snow, snow!

Elizabeth McDermott (9) St Nicholas' Middle School, Great Yarmouth

WINTER

I don't like the snow
It's cold sometimes,
And we have to go out,
And sometimes we fall,
On the black ice.

Children are playing in the
Snow.
Children are making men.
People chucking snowballs.

Daniel Hutchinson (9) St Nicholas' Middle School, Great Yarmouth

GRANNY SPIDER

Granny spider
Granny spider
Make, make a web,
A silver web.
Oh no, a spider
Ha, ha ha, a fly
To eat.

I've got my knife and fork,
You'd better fly away.
Spider wood-louse,
In your bed
Climbing up with your hairy legs.

Gavin Mutton (9) St Nicholas' Middle School, Great Yarmouth

THE COLOURFUL BUTTERFLY

I glide in the air,
And flutter too,
I'm very pleased I live near you,
I lay my eggs in my nest,
And most of all they love me best,
I love my butterfly just as you love me,
With all its colours it grows up with me.

Lorna Ferguson (9) St Nicholas' Middle School, Great Yarmouth

WINTER

Shivering, freezing,
  Snowing all day,
Snowballing,
  Snow down my back,
Making snowmen
  Most of the day.

Frozen ponds with ducks skidding,
  Old people stuck inside.

Children cold but happy to play,
  Ice skating down the lane,
Ice shining like glass,
  It's beautiful in the winter
      I like winter,
            Do you?

Rebecca Smith (9) St Nicholas' Middle School, Great Yarmouth

WINNIE THE WITCH

Ugly and green,
Fierce and frowning,
She glides through the air, her cape flows,
But she has never been seen.
A *mystery* everywhere.

Emma Ryan (9) St Nicholas' Middle School, Great Yarmouth

WINTER

Ice, ice, ice everywhere,
Snowing, snowing,
falling to the ground.

Ice is slidy,
It goes down
your back.

Slidy, slidy
Slidy everywhere,
Ducks sliding
everywhere too.

Ice down your chimney,
It is very very
cold!

Michael Moughton (9) St Nicholas' Middle School, Great Yarmouth

THE BUTTERFLY

Little butterfly, little butterfly,
In the breeze you fly,
With colours so bright as the sun in the sky,
So when you see the flower you like,
You can rest all day long.

Kristal Hodds (9) St Nicholas' Middle School, Great Yarmouth

THE SNAKE

Sssliding slithering slipping along.
Is the silent stealthy snake.
Colour yellow and black.
Twisting, curling, crushing prey.
Long and scaly.
Fangs so sharp,
Gliding hissing flicking his tongue
Is the silent stealthy snake!

David Jeal (10) St Nicholas' Middle School, Great Yarmouth

THE SNAKE

Stealthily sliding through the grass,
Waiting for the prey to pass,
Sometimes hiding in the trees,
Safely hidden by all the leaves,
A mouse comes creeping out of his hole,
The snake lunges at it and swallows it whole.

Claire-Louise Oakes (10) St Nicholas' Middle School, Great Yarmouth

SNAKES

The snake slithers and slides
Wrapping round a tree
Curling and twisting
Different coloured body
The snake is long
Thirty metres long
The snake is hissing and sliding along the floor
Gliding along the floor
Slithering and silent.

Donna Richardson (9) St Nicholas' Middle School, Great Yarmouth

HURRICANE

In the distant I can see it
coming
The rumbling, the howling, the
silent humming.
The houses are shaking,
people are waking.
Our house is blowing!
Where are we going?
People on the street are turning
around
Then they're being slowly lifted
off the ground.
In the distance I can see it
going
Now I can sit back and do
my sewing.

Jennifer Stacey (10) St Nicholas' Middle School, Great Yarmouth

THE DOVE

If a dove should
hover at thy window
grant it with kisses and hugs
It is I the dove.

If a dove should
hover at thy window
grant it helping and caring
It is I the dove.

Laura Watson (10) St Nicholas' Middle School, Great Yarmouth

THE JUNGLE

In the jungle
far away,
In Australia where the monkeys
play,
Monkey, monkey where are thee, swinging
from the biggest tree.

And on the tree who could there be,
but two little birds happily,
And on the ground, not making a sound
a mound of crocodiles, weighing hundreds
of pounds.

Leslie Doran (9) St Nicholas' Middle School, Great Yarmouth

THE JUNGLE

Spooky, scary, frightening,
Flies about your head.
You get that funny feeling, are
you here or in your bed?
Birds are singing sweetly,
and a lovely song they sing.

Trees are lurching above your head,
darkish greens and brown it
seems.
A snake slithers about your feet,
and a bright little thing he
was.

Victoria Hodds (9) St Nicholas' Middle School, Great Yarmouth

THE QUEST

Through dangly woods,
The aimless ooze,
A-dripping and a-dripping goes.
In twilight mist,
And steaming rain,
Adventures are afoot,
That's plain,
Scales and coils and yellow eyes,
Watch,
And wait,
And guard the prize.

David Kendall (10) St Nicholas' Middle School, Great Yarmouth

THE JUNGLE POEM

As I walk through the jungle
I hear the birds singing
Orange and black tigers
Walking in the mist.
Big, brown bears roaring in the sky.
Suddenly bang! Bang! Bang!
Little screams as the animals
Fall down dead.
The hunters get the animals
Then put them in vans,
Then drive off and leave the
Other animals in tears.
The large trees stand tall
As the moon shines down,
The animals curl up in their
Beds as they go to sleep.

Heidi Williams (10) St Nicholas' Middle School, Great Yarmouth

IN THE PARK

As I wandered through the park,
In the distance a dog began to bark,
In the trees the birds were singing
And the church bells were ringing,
All the squirrels in the trees,
Dancing about amongst the leaves,
Then the sun began to fall,
Quietness rested over all.

Samantha Kelly Eden (10) St Nicholas' Middle School, Great Yarmouth

THE SCARECROW

The scarecrow stands there
All alone.
Nobody likes him
Oh crows come here.

He's all alone
Nobody cares
He's not really scary
See him, come see him.

He stands alone late at night,
He has no bones,
Or even hands.
Come and see him
On this dark damp night.

Matthew Harvey (10) St Nicholas' Middle School, Great Yarmouth

SNAKES

Slithering and sliding
Hissing
Curls and twirls
Camouflage, red and green
Long and poisonous
Flickering his tongue
Shedding his skin
Danger! *Poisonous snake!*

Sarah Franklin (10) St Nicholas' Middle School, Great Yarmouth

THE DARK

I woke up one night
I needed the loo
But it was only half-past two.
I went down the stairs
The light wasn't on
I went in the bathroom
The bulb had gone
The shadows were lurking
I needed a drink
I was so scared I dared not blink
I went down the stairs
Holding my breath
I saw the bogey man
I was scared to death!
I gave out a scream
Mum turned on the light
'What's going on here?'
I gave mum a fright.

Hannah Catchpole (10) St Nicholas' Middle School, Great Yarmouth

RAIN

Drip, drip,
Splash, splash,
It's raining again,
I'm getting wet,
The wind's blowing,
My hair is tangling,
My eyes are watering,
I want to go home,
So run, run, run,
Yes, run all the way home.

Laura Jackson (10) St Nicholas' Middle School, Great Yarmouth

THE JELLY WOBBLE KISSER

It's fat.
It's wobbly.
It's out to catch you . . .
It's the *jelly wobble kisser.*
When you go out to sea
it's there.
If you see it row away
quick,
'cos its kiss will suck
you up and drench you
in spit, you had better
watch out it's the . . .
Jelly wobble kisser.

It's as big as a house
its lips are bigger than
Madonna's
(and redder!)
It's got red eyes
and its colour is orange.
So you had better watch
when you go to sea.
Beware!
Remember it will always
be there.

Gemma Cooper (9) St Nicholas' Middle School, Great Yarmouth

AUTUMN

In the autumn,
The harvest lady comes
All dressed in her wheat and corn!
Her beautiful jewellery sparkling!
Her crown made of lovely red poppies
Blackberries as the colour of her eyes.
Her faithful pets, the squirrel and the swallow!
Crunch! As she walks through the golden
Leaves. as she controls the autumn.

Kelly Warnes (9) St Nicholas' Middle School, Great Yarmouth

AUTUMN

In autumn leaves fly away
With the wind.
Leaves, leaves everywhere
Even in your hair
Round the houses
When they go the wind
Goes too.
They play cops and robbers
With the wind.
In the harvest, leaves turn
Into gold.
Squirrels dance on leaves.

Scott Jonas (10) St Nicholas' Middle School, Great Yarmouth

THE FLY

I saw a big fat fly one day it had big
wings and flew away.
I caught a glimpse of
its lovely
colours.
It was
blue, and green.
It landed
on a fence
and turned
around.
It had
six legs
and a
fat velvet
body.
It raised
its wings
and . . . flew away!

Paul Kitchen (9) St Nicholas' Middle School, Great Yarmouth

SNAILS

So slimy
So horrible
Long eyes
So it can see where it's going
Hard shell
So revolting
No matter how much you shout it takes its time
Why is a snail so slow?

Christopher Merkis (9) St Nicholas' Middle School, Great Yarmouth

JUNGLE

I walk down the jungle,
I hear not a word,
but birds singing
as loud as can be
I see a big snake
with lots of colours
on his long back.
There are lots of big long trees
with loud little and big monkeys
I'm going home.

Emma K Squirrell (9) St Nicholas' Middle School, Great Yarmouth

FOX

A fox walking
in the dark night,
Staring with his narrow
green eyes,
His wet black nose
sniffing the air,
His long ears listen
for squeaking mice,
He sits and waits
for lunch,
Suddenly he twitches
his ear,
He curves his neck
and looks at a bush,
He creeps to the bush
and pounces at his prey.

Glen Banham (10) St Nicholas' Middle School, Great Yarmouth

HURRICANE

I heard something. Oh no
I cried!
Howling through the windows
I am scared. Whistling through
the keyhole.
House lifting up, roof blown off,
letterbox clattering, rubbish
blowing around, trees rustling
on the wall.

All clear at last!

Laura Smith (10) St Nicholas' Middle School, Great Yarmouth

AUTUMN

Autumn leaves,
fall from the trees,
Leaves crackle and crunch,
while squirrels munch nuts.

Leaves turn brown,
with a reddish tan,
The sky turns cold and misty,
Soon the day is gone.

Elizabeth Stacey (10) St Nicholas' Middle School, Great Yarmouth

IN THE WINTER

In the winter,
It is very cold
And when we go out we wear
A hat to keep our ears warm
A coat to keep our bodies warm
A pair of gloves to keep our hands warm
A scarf to keep our neck warm.

When it's very very cold
Our fingers go all numb
And when we get warmer we get
Pins and needles in our feet.

It's nice when snowflakes come down
Because it looks pretty.

Heidi Judd (9) St Nicholas' Middle School, Great Yarmouth

THE BOMBS

I was in my Anderson shelter.
A bomb dropped on my Anderson shelter.
My baby brother Jake was crying.
I thought my house was bombed.
I was scared.
I heard a bomb blow up.
I didn't like it.

Emily Wenham (8) St Nicholas' Middle School, Great Yarmouth

JAMES AND THE GIANT PEACH

Look at that funny thin black thing gliding
through the water over there.
There are two of them!
There are lots of them
They must be some kind of fish.
They are sharks cried the earthworm.
I just know they are sharks
Sharks who were crushing slowly around and around
the peach.
Just assuming that they are sharks,
One of those thin black fins suddenly
Changed direction.
They all watched aghast.
There must have been twenty or thirty of them at
Least.

Samantha Mason (9) St Nicholas' Middle School, Great Yarmouth

TREES

Trees are being cut down.
Animals running away.
They are scared and frightened.
Some are alive and dying.
Asleep, awake.
Wake up.
Quick the forest is being chopped down.
To the work men.
Where's my home?
Where's my friends?
Go away.
Or I'll burn you,
And kill you.

Linzi Williams (9) St Nicholas' Middle School, Great Yarmouth

WATCH OUT MR FOX

Caterpillar tractors,
Murderous, brutal looking monsters.
Bean shouted
Death to the fox!
Under the big tree.
Rocks were sent flying.
Rocks falling.
The noise was deafening,
Terrible clanging and banging.
What are they doing?
It's an earthquake,
Said Mr Fox.
Our tunnel's getting shorter.
It's only a few feet away from us now!
'Tractors,'
Shouted Mr Fox.
'Dig for your lives!
Dig! Dig! Dig!'

Stewart McGovern (9) St Nicholas' Middle School, Great Yarmouth

SNOWMAN

Snowman
Made of snow
Eyes of charcoal
Mouth of stones
Carrot for nose,
Hat and scarf to keep him warm
Children made him round and tall
But when the sun came out
All that was left of him was a big puddle of water.

Thomas Bristo (9) St Nicholas' Middle School, Great Yarmouth

SNAIL

A snail is slow
A snail is slippery
A snail is slimy
A snail has got a shell
A snail is small
A snail is slithering
A snail is disgusting
A snail is soft.

Asa Skitterall (9) St Nicholas' Middle School, Great Yarmouth

BEES

As fast as a bee
quietly as a worm
scurrying, hurrying
backwards and forwards
all day long
as a bee, as a bee, as a bee
collecting honey
all day long
for his queen.

Lee Hammond (9) St Nicholas' Middle School, Great Yarmouth

DESTROYING THE FOREST

In the forest it is nice
Lots of leaves and trees.
Logs on the ground.
Beautiful animals
Brother birds.
Slithering snakes.
Jumping frogs.

Now chopping down trees
Killing the forest.
Polluting water.

Harrison Puckett (8) St Nicholas' Middle School, Great Yarmouth

IN THE ANDERSON SHELTER

Children screaming
Sirens go
People hear bomb - dropping
People cold and damp
Lights in the sky
People worried
Hear thud
People squashed
Very small
People crying.

Nina Ingram (8) St Nicholas' Middle School, Great Yarmouth

SNAILS

Slowly but quietly the snail crawls.
Along with his house.
How long do I have to carry my house?
I may be slow, but why do I have
To carry my house with
Me?
I am now
going up the wall
with my house
to the green grass to
have some food,
I am nearly here now I
better hurry.

Kelly Anderson (8) St Nicholas' Middle School, Great Yarmouth

SNAILS

Slowly but quiet, shuffling along,
carrying his house up the wall,
Snails are not very small.
Going to the green grass to have a picnic.
Snails are greedy
but snails are not speedy.
While they sleep in the soil
not a sound he makes.
In the morning he awakes
then back to bed.
Don't forget there's a day ahead.

Siân Hughes (8) St Nicholas' Middle School, Great Yarmouth

AIR RAID

Siren sounding,
Children screaming,
Guns firing,
And bombs dropping.
Down in the Anderson shelter
Hear bombs thud,
Damp and cold,
Oxygen short,
With little food,
The war went on,
But one day I thought I was killed,
House blown up, mum went up,
Saw a German pilot
Shooting bullets through the Anderson shelter
Saw mum in the air,
Quick get her.
Krrrrrr I'm dead.

Nicholas Hodds (9) St Nicholas' Middle School, Great Yarmouth

THE BUTTERFLY

It was a little egg.
Then it hatched.
A little hairy caterpillar,
got fatter and fatter.
It made a cocoon.
On a sunny day a beautiful butterfly,
appears.
Colourful and light.

Brett Henderson (9) St Nicholas' Middle School, Great Yarmouth

RAIN FORESTS BEING DESTROYED

Trees trees save our trees
Trees getting cut down
Rain forests flooded
Birds flying away
Animals dying
People polluting rivers
Evergreen leaves turning to dust
Carbon Dioxide spreading in the air.
Soil dries up and washes away.
Trees falling to the ground.

Ian Anjos (9) St Nicholas' Middle School, Great Yarmouth

TRACTORS

The enormous caterpillar tractors
Mechanical shovels
Black
Brutal looking monsters.
Death to the fox
Biting huge mouth full of soil
First place
Flying trees
The noise was deafening
It's an earthquake
Huge black tractors.
Dig for your lives. *Dig, dig dig!*

Toni Underwood (9) St Nicholas' Middle School, Great Yarmouth

DOWN AT THE POND

Lee the worm
he comes out
every term
and when
we dug
the garden
up we
found
lots more
other worms
so we took
them in to
meet their
new friends.

Dion Carr (8) St Nicholas' Middle School, Great Yarmouth

CREEPY CRAWLIES

Creepy crawlies,
In my bed.
Creepy crawlies,
On my shelf.
Creepy crawlies,
In my bath.
Creepy crawlies,
Everywhere!

Emma Barwick (9) St Nicholas' Middle School, Great Yarmouth

BANG!

The war went on
People suffering
Children screaming!
Bombs dropping
Then bang!
House blown up.
Someone came down
The stairs rolling
     Dead.
Guns firing siren going off
Then thud a bomb bounced.
Then bang! Anderson shelter gone
Damp and cold in shelter
No food!
All gone, Germans still
Went on.

Sara Moore (9) St Nicholas' Middle School, Great Yarmouth

COMING OUT OF THE FOG

It was a dark and gloomy night.
It was a very scary night.
There was something coming out of the fog.
The fog was very grey and gloomy.
I was scared.
It sounded like Darth Vader,
But it was white and tall.
It had a big nose and was thin.
It had big big teeth and they were dirty.
And it had a big chin,.
Pity I couldn't see it again.

Luke Child (10) St Thomas More RC Middle School, Norwich

ALL WAS QUIET UNTIL

All was quiet until
The sirens were screaming,
I was not dreaming,
The world war was on.

Outside was chaos,
Everyone was running,
Bombs were coming,
The world war was on.

No time to think,
The children were crying,
People were dying,
The world war was on.

Flames lit the sky,
Buildings had collapsed,
Which only left gaps,
The world war was on.

Peter Willson (11) St Thomas More RC Middle School, Norwich

LOOKING THROUGH A MOLE HOLE

Looking through a mole hole, I can see . . .
A worm digging through the soil.
Looking through a mole hole, I can see . . .
A mole with a shiny black button nose
A jutting out face like the point of a pencil.
His fur is like the navy cotton of my jumper.
And the eyes are closed
Like a crack in the wall.

Dominic Burke (8) St Thomas More RC Middle School, Norwich

ALL WAS QUIET UNTIL

All was quiet and peaceful,
The beautiful lake sparkled in the glowing evening sun,
The fleece white swans swam more gracefully than ever,
The sweet chirping of birds was carried over the lake by the cool breeze,
Little children ran about with bare feet in the cool green grass,
The tall trees were dancing in the cool summer breeze.
It was oh so quiet until . . .

The trees were cut down,
The litter was spread,
The animals were killed
And the cars drove across,
The birds were shot,
Houses were built,
The factories puffed smoke,
All destroying the beautiful lake.
Is this what we want?
Is this what we need?
Is this all we do?
I'll leave it with you!

Victoria Young (11) St Thomas More RC Middle School, Norwich

IT CAME OUT OF THE FOG

The fog like a black cloak,
The fog like a blindfold.
Eyes are all around me,
It's getting rather cold.

An icy finger ran down my spine.
It's not very nice to be alone in the night.
Look at me, I'm shivering with fright,
It's getting rather scary.

It's looming up, a giant shape,
The eyes flashing brightly.
Fading away, almost gone.
It's getting rather clear.

Suzanne Balcombe (9) St Thomas More RC Middle School, Norwich

LOOKING THROUGH GRANDMA'S WINDOW

I am looking through grandma's window
This is what I can see
The wide sea like a blanket on a giant's bed.
In the background rocks tall like soldiers
ready for a battle.
Up above my head puffins like grand men
with their smart clean jackets on.

On the sand is seaweed like
a green slimy snake.
There, on the rocks, a lighthouse stands tall and
proud like it is the boss of the sea.
I will look out of the window tomorrow.

Monica Mason (9) St Thomas More RC Middle School, Norwich

IT CAME OUT OF THE FOG . . .

It came out of the fog
The haze of a fog
Almost wrapping itself round
The shape, like a
Blanket of cloud
Covering the land.

If you run, you can't
Escape it,
Following, following
Not frightening
But mysterious.

Like a cave without
An end,
The shape was
Distorted but I could
See it coming towards
Me, the fog was stuffy
And I was sweating.

The damp vapour made it
Feel like rain,
It was so thick now I
Couldn't see my hand.
The shape disappears.

Joshua Kaye (10) St Thomas More RC Middle School, Norwich

LOOK THROUGH A WINDOW

When you look through a window
You will see flowers standing proudly
With their big tall stalks
And beautiful leaves.
When you look through a window
You might see a unicorn with its white mane
And its lovely golden horn
Galloping on the hill tops.
When you look through a window
You will see children with the armbands on
And playing with their snorkels and masks.
When you look through a window
You might see pixies in their little green hats
and coats.
And trousers with a brown belt and gold
buckle.

Michael Kerridge (8) St Thomas More RC Middle School, Norwich

LOOKING THROUGH A PAIR OF BINOCULARS

Looking through a pair of binoculars . . .
I can see . . .
A busy street with tall buildings.
Cars moving and stopping at the lights.
People hurrying everywhere.
Looking through a pair of binoculars
I can see . . .
Mountains with snow on the top.
Tall trees with claws.
Two busy squirrels
getting ready for winter.

Aaron Bradley (9) St Thomas More RC Middle School, Norwich

LOOKING THROUGH MY BEDROOM KEYHOLE

Look through my bedroom keyhole
What do you see?
Me, playing on my Megadrive, quietly.
Look through my bedroom keyhole
What do you see?
My sister creeping in, nervously.
Look through my bedroom keyhole
What do you see?
My sister annoying me, *loudly!*
Look through my bedroom keyhole
What do you see?
Me saying to my sister 'Push off!' Angrily.
Look through my bedroom keyhole
What do you see?
Me playing with my Lego, peacefully.
Look through my bedroom keyhole
What do you see?
Me asleep, softly.

Alexander Holland (9) St Thomas More RC Middle School, Norwich

MY IMAGINATION

Sometimes the sea is as red as a ruby.
Sometimes the sun never rises.
Sometimes the planet Mars is brighter than the sun.
Sometimes the world goes round the moon.
Sometimes the clouds are as soft as a cat.
Sometimes I can feel the trees and plants.
Sometimes the grass is as hard as steel.
Sometimes I travel to the future.
Sometimes UFOs land in my garden
Sometimes my shadow runs.

Shaun Hunton (9) St Thomas More RC Middle School, Norwich

IT CAME OUT OF THE MIST

Mist is swirling around me,
The lake is calm and barely seen.
The hoot of an owl is occasionally heard
The thick musty air feels draughty.

Mist is tangling in my hair,
The waves crashing against the rocks
There is something arriving here,
It looks long mighty and giant.

The whale has gleaming white eyes,
It sounds like an engine
At last the fog is clearing
It is a gigantic submarine with lights.

Joseph Clark (10) St Thomas More RC Middle School, Norwich

IT CAME OUT OF THE MIST

I walked through the woods as the mist came down
So I sat down and couldn't admire the lake,
The glacier dipped from its overhanging ledge
and the lake was hard to see.

A hand came out of the grey water but didn't move a muscle
its fingers were dark as death
It grabbed me and pulled me
into the water.

I could hear waves gently lapping the pebbles
I could hear the wind gently blow the trees.
I slowly went under the water and down and down.

Andrew Snowling (10) St Thomas More RC Middle School, Norwich

IT CAME OUT OF THE FOG

I'm looking out of my bedroom window,
It's foggy outside again.
But today there is something different about the fog,
It looks like something very big is out there.

Oh my goodness, it looks like a tiger,
With big green gloomy eyes looking at me.
I think it might be growling but I can't hear anything.
It's the fog, so spooky you would think it was magical.

The fog can sometimes play tricks with your eyes,
But it is not playing tricks with my eyes.
There is something out there and it has got big green eyes.
Maybe it's a wolf with its big long misty tail.

It's coming closer and closer. *It's a a a a a a . . .*
Oh, it's only our cat.

Rachel Loughlin (10) St Thomas More RC Middle School, Norwich

OUT OF THE MIST

I was standing at the sea when the mist came down
The mist was like a kettle boiling.
Slowly surrounding me.
I was alone.

A ghostly shadow came towards me
It was then I shouted 'Help,'
It's trying to kill me.
It's coming closer.

I saw a fin.
It was speeding at me.
But it was then I saw
A mini submarine.

Stuart White (10) St Thomas More RC Middle School, Norwich

ALL WAS QUIET UNTIL . . .

I was just sitting down listening
And I felt something run up my spine
It was one of those silly words again
Oh no! It was getting higher
Bigger and bigger
Mrs Cass was talking about silence
That made it even worse
Bigger and bigger
Higher and higher -
It was on my tongue
Couldn't hold it in -
Oh no!
Yabbadabbadoooo!
The whole class looked at me
I could just hear Mrs Cass
'All was quiet until . . . you!'

Rosemary Bool (11) St Thomas More RC Middle School, Norwich

IT CAME OUT OF THE MIST

The swirling grey, the blinding mist,
Damp and cold, creepy and wet.
Stale air, breathless gasps,
Blurry sights eerie noise.

A hovering figure, a flapping sound,
A green face, some evil eyes,
Black cape flowing, cackling laugh,
Thirsting for blood all the time.

Now the mist is clearing up,
I can see what it is,
It's an owl that lost his way,
In the gloomy fog today.

Martin Race (10) St Thomas More RC Middle School, Norwich

LOOK THROUGH A WINDOW

Look through a window and you will see
A massive cargo ship
Look through a window and you might see
Some nasty pirates robbing other rich ships
Look through a window and you will see
Brave people swimming far out
Look through a window and you might see
Mermaids combing their hair
Look through a window and you will see
Some tired seagulls flapping their wings
Look through a window and you might see
A fierce dragon swooping up and down
Look through a window and you will see
Mum coming upstairs . . .

Uh-oh! *Got to go!*

Juliet Goymer (8) St Thomas More RC Middle School, Norwich

IT CAME OUT OF THE MIST

Like spirits from the deep the dark mist was rising
Then it buttoned its thick fur coat
It felt as damp and airless as the ocean
It was grey just like a ghost.

Like a trickle of water I heard a noise
A dark flying shadow in the sky
I just felt as if I was going to die
A flying eyeball on the film of mist

It started to make a squeaking noise
It looked like a vampire bat
Its wings opened so did its mouth,
Then it flew away.

Patrick Maguire (10) St Thomas More RC Middle School, Norwich

IT CAME OUT OF THE MIST

I was in a misty wood without my friends,
There was cloudy whiteness around all the bends
Which way should I go? Which way should I hide?
In the crowded trees of the wood.

There's peculiar noises, in the dark wood,
I'd run away if I could - but I can't.
There was a strange shuffling noise coming from a tree,
But with all this fog, I couldn't really see.

There in the mist, a figure stood,
I'm not sure if I should -
But I took a step forward.
Crack! Went a branch,
Something appeared.

Its ears pricked up,
Feet shaped like a cup,
Tail like a knife
Whiskers lit up,
Shiny nose,
Toes curled in,
Teeth locked together.
A fox peered out, looked around, and scampered off.

Jennifer Martin (10) St Thomas More RC Middle School, Norwich

ALL WAS QUIET UNTIL . . .

Bombs hurtle from the sky,
lots of people just drop and die,
I hear people shout,
I hear people yell the bombs let out a toxic
smell.
I hear sounds of terror as people scream,
planes rush by
they're horrible machines,
I hope people learn a lesson from this,
while tyres burn,
engines hiss.
I hate this war I always will.
Then all was quiet all was still

Until . . .

Jessica Anderton (10) St Thomas More RC Middle School, Norwich

IT CAME OUT OF THE MIST

I saw a small island on the horizon,
Tall slim trees swaying in the calm wind,
Bright lanterns glaring out through the mist,
Strange smells of rotting fish.

As the sea rumbled up the beach,
Out of the misty haze of the sea,
The island grew fainter,
As the mist grew thicker.
Then the island turned away.

The mist is clearing like a sheet.
Sunlight beams coming down
On this misty land.
The waves are calm, no smell of fish.
But no more island and no more mist.

Thomas Arthurton (10) St Thomas More RC Middle School, Norwich

ALL WAS QUIET UNTIL

I was having a family chat with mum,
And all was quiet until . . .
We hear the air raid signal
we run, too late!
Mum kept running
I was stuck under the rubble,
I think mum's made it,
only my hand is showing
I hear the bell of the fire engine
they are scratching at the rubble
babies are crying in full volume
I hear the whistle of a bomb

silence

Who's that over there
under the rubble?
It's mum!
Please not mum
I shout at the firemen,
'Over there, it's my mum.'
They don't hear me

Bang!

Mum's dead.

Emily Joy (11) St Thomas More RC Middle School, Norwich

IT CAME OUT OF THE MIST

I could feel the cold of the sudden mist.
It tingled a bit but I didn't care.
I could smell the murky polluted river.
A milky wave swirling around me.

In front of me was a blurry shape.
It looked like a bull but bulls are too big.
It howled, I panicked, what was that?
It had huge blood-stained teeth that
It was going to dig into me.

It had a large pink nose.
And sharp pointy ears like bread knives.
It had a great big slobbering tongue.
To lick my bones clean.

It bit my shoe and I hit the earth with a bump.
It licked my face it's going to eat me.
Hey I recognise that slobber.
It's Bruno my pet dog he's come to
Save me from the fog.

Gemma Girdlestone : St Thomas More RC Middle School, Norwich

THE GOLDFISH

Looking through the clean tank glass,
Wondering what is going on.
All is as quiet as a mouse.
The fish is hungry,
Where is his food?
All is getting mysterious now,
If only the fish had known
That his owner had died.
Who shall feed him now?
The fish has the darkest of feelings.
Two weeks later the water is as black as coal.
The fish is dying,
Now the fish meets his friend again.

Joseph Rutland (8) St Thomas More RC Middle School, Norwich

ALL WAS QUIET UNTIL . . .

All was quiet until . . .
A low drone is heard above,
It gets louder.
It gets nearer.
Everyone runs for shelter,
There's chaos in the streets.
Screaming!
Shouting!
Children crying 'Mum'.
Then silence.

They freeze.
They know.
The *doodlebug* has come.

Sophie Wright (11) St Thomas More RC Middle School, Norwich

LOOKING THROUGH

The long, narrow street
Is as quiet as a small fluffy mouse.
There are shadows as the warm lights of the houses
Shine down into the streets.
The tall, white houses
Stand out against the dark, wet background,
Like a black cat in snow.
The small child walks cold and tired,
Like someone who hasn't slept for two long
Nights.
A small light hangs on one wall
It is quite dim,
The only light on the street.
The puddles splash out at his feet,
Like a fox pouncing on a rabbit.
The boy is tired from a long day at school.
He drags his feet slowly home.

James Young (9) St Thomas More RC Middle School, Norwich

ALL WAS QUIET UNTIL . . .

The wail of the sirens, now it all begins,
Wardens grab their helmets of tin,
Directing the people to shelters within.
The drone of approaching planes in the sky,
Means terror and fear to people nearby.

The guns return fire, the sky is alight,
And people are praying they'll live through this night,
Friendships begin out of hope and the fear,
They murmur 'Thank God' when they hear *the all clear.*

Rubble is all that remains of some homes,
To others they now have become tombs.
Digging and searching for a glimmer of life,
Success is not measured in labour or strife!

The sun shining down, a new day at last,
Hopefully soon this war will be past,
Children are playing - hear the birds singing
And all once again, enjoy life - meant for living!

Kay Field (11) St Thomas More RC Middle School, Norwich

ALL WAS QUIET UNTIL . . .

The sirens wailed the *all clear*
The drone of engines was now a forgotten
memory.
The boy stumbled across the rubble
A dirty bruised hand stuck up from the dirt.
'Mummy, mummy.' Was that her ring?
He scrambled searching for her face
and found it.
The look in her eyes was frozen still
He reached out and touched her face
It was cold.
Suddenly he is running.
He doesn't know who is screaming.

Mark Haydn (11) St Thomas More RC Middle School, Norwich

THE STORM

The cool breeze, the splashing sea
The loneliness surrounds me.
The misty air, the cold wind
As dark clouds rise above me.
The thunder starts to roll
The lightning starts to clash
The wind is howling and
The oceans start to roar
Then everything turns silent
Not a sound or a movement.

Kimberley Mclaren (8) West Winch CP School

DESERTED ISLAND

A deserted island would do for me,
I would sit under the shade of the coconut tree,
I would sit on the beach under the sun,
This is my place for having fun!
Laughter and fun would fill the air,
Some grown-ups here to love and to care,
I'd love to build a fabulous raft,
Some hideout places a hidden shaft,
A tent to go out and camp with,
A deserted island my place to live.

Sam Wells (9) West Winch CP School

HIDING

Let's play hide and seek,
I'll count, but don't peek,
Now where shall I hide?
Maybe inside.
Oh help! She's coming,
I'd better start running,
I'll hide in the shed,
No under the bed,
So under the bed I dive,
I'm amazed, I am still alive,
I think I'm going to sneeze.
It's the pollen in the summer breeze,
Atishoo! Game's up she cries, I've found you!

Nicola Symonds (9) West Winch CP School

MY CAT

My cat is called Tabitha.
She is the worst cat mum ever met.
Tabitha is the second best to me.
Tabitha is mainly white.
She has black and orange stripes and spots.
She is a tortoise-shell cat.
She is the fastest in the family.
Tabitha is the champion of the world at catching
mice.

Luke Allen (7) Wormegay RC Primary School

MY DOG

My dog is called Jasper
I think he's nearly as fast as a greyhound.
He always does what I tell him to do.
Every night he comes upstairs and sleeps in my bedroom.
He's nice to cuddle.
In the garden he chases little birds.
In the field he runs around his track chasing cars.
When he catches a ball he does a somersault.

Paul Harrod (10) Wormegay RC Primary School

DREAMS

Dreams are funny things.
You never know who you are, where you are,
Or whether you are dreaming or not
When you wake up you know all this information.
I've never understood what dreams are.
I have a theory they are magical stretches of imagination,
That stretch for miles and miles,
Once you have walked those miles you wake up,
And start a new day.
There is a never-ending list of things along that stretch.
Others believe different,
But I believe what I believe and nobody can stop me.

Edward Allen (9) Wormegay RC Primary School

MY ROCK

My rock reminds me of ice being chipped.
It looks like an arrow in the rock.
It appears to look like some glass.
It is shaped like a diamond.
I think it looks like a snowstorm.

Luke Chopping (8) Wormegay RC Primary School

BONFIRE

The flames look like hot tongues licking
the wood.
The ash which flies up looks like orange
butterflies.
The crackling sounds like my car on a cold
morning.
The sparks fly like fireworks in the night
sky.
The flames dance among the wood
The fire sizzles like a witch's cauldron.

Graham Britton (9) Wormegay RC Primary School

BEDTIME AND MORNING

When I go to bed
Dad tucks me in
All of a sudden the light goes dim
It sounds as if the toys get up and
move about.
But I don't stay awake to find out.
In the morning it looks the same, as if nothing
had ever happened.
But I know different.

Amanda Arndt (11) Wormegay RC Primary School

MY BEDROOM

My bedroom looks like a rubbish bin
Rolling and rolling about.
My bean bag rustles like the wind outside
The clothes are scattered like a mosaic
I feel that I am in the safest place in the world
When I'm in my bedroom.

Naomi Harrod (9) Wormegay RC Primary School

VOLCANO

Fiery hot
Smoky
A devil's home
Only a big bang can show
The evil light that it keeps inside.
It mountains over the world
It destroys anything
With its deadly gases
Pompeii knows what it can do
With its hot and boiling lava
Living in the shadow of a volcano
Can be a source of
Constant fear.

Oliver Parker (10) Wormegay RC Primary School

MY GARDEN

It is all quiet in my garden
I feel like I'm in my very own world
The flowers look like crowds of people
All crammed together
Watching me.
The place I dare not hide in
is our shed
At the bottom of our garden.
It's all dark and dusty
With glass and cobwebs
It's all creepy in there
I'm happy where I am in the trees
Behind the bushes
In my very own world
I don't want to go in there because
I think I'll be taken to a creepy world
And never come back
And someone else shall take the special world
I left behind.

Rosie Moeser (10) Wormegay RC Primary School

I LIKE . . .

. . . Aeroplanes gliding through the sky
. . . Cats purring all night and day.
. . . Rabbits our rabbit is afraid of us.
. . . Ducks floating all day or plodding.
. . . Geese hissing or honking like mad.
. . . Fish gormlessly floating deep under the waves.
. . . Mice scrambling away looking for food.
. . . Hens wandering around in farms and fields
. . . Frogs hopping about and swimming.
. . . Cars zooming about on roads.

Robert Squires (9) Wormegay RC Primary School

INFORMATION

We hope you have enjoyed reading this book - and that you will continue to enjoy it in the coming years.

If you like reading and writing poetry drop us a line, or give us a call, and we'll send you a free information pack.

Write to

Poetry Now (Young Writers) Information
1-2 Wainman Road
Woodston
Peterborough
PE2 7BU